FROM SPOKESMAN TO PRESS SECRETARY:
White House Media Operations

William C. Spragens
The American University
Bowling Green State University

with

Carole Ann Terwoord

University Press of America™

560195

Library of Congress Catalog Card Number: 80-8296

TO ELAINE

iii

ACKNOWLEDGMENTS

This book would not have been possible without the aid of many individuals and institutions. I am particularly indebted to the Press Secretaries themselves who made themselves available for interviews—these included Pierre Salinger and George Christian, and Bill Moyers consented to provide information as did Jody Powell. I am also indebted to the American Broadcasting Company for use of a brief portion of a "Good Morning America" interview with Ronald Nessen. I am especially indebted to Bruce Hagerty of ABC for continuing cooperation in various articles and portions of books I have written about his father, James C. Hagerty. The proffered assistance of Jerald terHorst should not be overlooked; I am also appreciative of Dom Bonafede's permission to quote from his Washington Journalism Review interview with Ronald Ziegler.

Grants from the Lyndon Baines Johnson Foundation and the Bowling Green State University Faculty Research Committee facilitated research on the Press Office at the Dwight D. Eisenhower Library, Abilene, Kansas; the John F. Kennedy Library, Boston, and the Lyndon Baines Johnson Library, Austin, Texas. In addition, the National Archives staff was kind enough to permit me to view audio-visual materials regarding news conferences. Here a special word of thanks is due Brenda Beasley, archivist, and James Holzhouser, who is in charge of the Ford collection. Work with the Vanderbilt Archives on network newscasts from the month of September 1978 gave valuable insights into the Carter media relations at the time of Camp David, as did an earlier interview completed with Barry Jagoda, former television adviser to President Carter.

I am also appreciative of the encouragement of the Presidency Research Group of the American Political Science Association. Colleagues who have shared their own work with me or who have

v

been cooperative in other ways include the follow-ing specialists on the American Presidency: Fred I. Greenstein; Dorothy B. James; R. Gordon Hoxie; Thomas E. Cronin; Bruce Buchanan; Kenneth E. Davison; Stephen Wayne; Michael Robinson.

I also appreciate the opportunity to work with the press office at the Democratic National Committee as a part of the staff from September to December 1978, and more recently for the cooperation and assistance of Robert Neuman, Democratic National Committee press secretary, and two former students who are now staff members there--Kim Brenner and Cindy Myers. I am also appreciative to Chairman John White, Elaine Kamarck of the Platform Committee staff of the DNC, former political director John Rendon, former research director Scott Wolf, and librarian Frank Bierlein for their part in enriching my insights into the way in which issues are dealt with by the White House Press Office.

Former White House staff members have been of assistance, including Arthur Schlesinger Jr., Myer Feldman, Walt W. Rostow, and such persons as Carolyn Shields of Mr. Powell's office.

A good deal of gratitude must be reserved for present and former Washington correspondents who have co-operated in this project, including Frank Cormier of the Associated Press, Robert Pierpoint and Bob Schieffer of CBS, Judy Woodruff and Tom Brokaw of NBC, Ann Compton of ABC, Hedrick Smith of the New York _Times_, and Marquis Childs, the columnist. I appreciate the helpfulness of Joseph Kraft as well. NBC granted special permission to quote from a copyrighted documentary narrated by David Brinkley.

I am most appreciative of the work as an editorial assistant, stenographer and picture editor, by Carole Terwoord, who contributed immensely to the timely publication of this work, as well as the work of Stacie Konecny who typed an earlier draft,

and Tammy Manahan, who compiled the index. Wilma
Konecny was most helpful in earlier stages of the
project. Others who helped at any stage including
Lori Mizer, Cathy Anne Miller, Stacie Pellegrino,
Beth Markley and Isabelle Notar must be thanked.

Special gratitude goes to colleagues who aided
my work at various stages including William O.
Reichert, political science chair at BGSU; Emil
Dansker of the BGSU School of Journalism; Ronald
Etzel of the BGSU Research Services Office; James
Bissland of the BGSU School of Journalism, and
Jerone Stephens and Dennis Anderson who have
helped stimulate an atmosphere conducive to research at my home base, as well as David Brown,
executive director of the Washington Semester
Program at the American University who has provided an opportunity for me to share my research
with students from all over the nation.

The patience and encouragement of my wife
Elaine have been of .the utmost help in the completion of this project and this work is dedicated
to her.

To any others unmentioned I also am grateful.
J. E. Lyons and Helen Hudson of University Press of
America have been most helpful in the production
and planning of this book.

All errors are my own responsibility, as well
as the interpretations which are mine alone.

                              W. C. S.
                              Bowling Green, Ohio
        August 1980   Washington

TABLE OF CONTENTS

TABLE OF ILLUSTRATIONS

This work grew out of an earlier volume, <u>The</u>
<u>Presidency</u> <u>and</u> <u>the</u> <u>Mass</u> <u>Media</u> <u>in</u> <u>the</u> <u>Age</u> <u>of</u>
<u>Television</u>, in which I devoted a single chapter to
the White House Press Secretaries, with particular
attention to James C. Hagerty. At that point it
seemed they play such a vital role on the White
House staff that a close-up look was necessary.

The other work in this field by Michael
Grossman and Joyce Kumar is excellent, and I have
been fortunate to be able to combine the interest
in this topic with a wider-ranging interest in the
White House staff which has provided contributions
to the work of Bradley Nash and the publications
of the Center for the Study of the Presidency. I
hope this book supplements material I have written
for volumes by Dr. Nash and by William C. Adams of
the Television and Politics Study Center at the
George Washington University.

Three perspectives are used in analyzing the
Press Office. These are the use of essentially
biographical material about the Press Secretaries
themselves, supplemented by interviews where
possible. The second is an effort to see the
Press Secretaries as their White House colleagues
saw or see them. Finally I wanted to get a
correspondents-eye view of the Press Secretaries.
The concluding portion of the book is an overview
of this important office.

CHAPTER ONE

INTRODUCTION: WHITE HOUSE MEDIA OPERATIONS AND

THEIR RISE IN IMPORTANCE WITH MODERN MEDIA

Media Relations as a Focal Point in the
White House--During the 1970's and 1980's, relations between the Presidency and the mass media
have made the White House Press Office a focal
point of attention.

The institutional relationship between the
mass communications media and the White House has
become a crucial one.[1] In previous research, I
referred to the White House Press Secretary as
the one person who stands at the intersection, or
interface, of these two institutions. The Press
Secretary interprets the President and his activities to the news media; he also gives the President an idea what the news media want to know
about the President.

An interview with Frank Cormier, senior Associated Press correspondent, and another interview with Pierre Salinger, Press Secretary during
the Kennedy Administration, confirmed from actual
experience observations made about the evolution
of the media coverage of the White House. The
basic trend during the period between 1960 and
1980 has been the evolution of the media from

---

[1]Barry Jagoda, former television adviser to
President Carter, felt that "institutional dynam-
ics between the media as an institution and the
White House as an institution" were most important. See William C. Spragens, The Presidency and
the Mass Media in the Age of Television (Washington: University Press of America, 1978), p. 290.

1

dominance by newspapers to an era of networks and cable television.[2]

The print media--newspapers and magazines, primarily--were still dominant in 1960 even though television was fast rising and had been on the national scene since the coast-to-coast telecast of the Japanese peace treaty signing in 1951 following the completion of the coaxial cable link. This change took place gradually, and sample survey reports indicated that in the late 1960's, around 1967, audiences began to report greater reliance on television than on newspapers for basic news. During this time, the interpretive, "backgrounding" role of newspapers also increased enormously. An interview with Robert Pierpoint of CBS News also indicated that he feels there has been a great growth of professionalism during these two decades.[3]

It's significant that while television is dominant in national reporting of White House news, the Washington community referred to by Richard Neustadt relies heavily on newspapers, especially the Washington Post and New York Times. Also the Washington Star and other East Coast newspapers including the Baltimore Sun and Boston Globe, comment heavily and frequently on national affairs.

There is another politically important point. The increase in importance of cable television has followed the reverse of the oft-repeated cycle of diffusion of new technology. In the case of cable television, small mountain towns in Pennsylvania were among the first to use what was known as community antenna cable television. It spread to

---

[2]Personal interview with Pierre Salinger, ABC Paris Bureau, 22 Avenue d'Eylau, Paris, September 18, 1979; telephone interview with Frank Cormier, Washington, July 18, 1979. Both interviews are quoted more extensively later in this book.

[3]Telephone interview with Pierpoint, August 6, 1979.

smaller communities in more isolated regions as a means of boosting and improving the over-the-air signals of major stations. The final stage in introduction of cable TV technology has now apparently been reached, with first medium-sized cities and now larger cities such as New York and Chicago benefiting from new cable systems. All of these factors magnify the image of the President, good or bad, as viewed in the living rooms of the American public. The 100% "wired nation" may never occur, but cable technology is now spreading rapidly. Wider use of satellites and fiberoptics technology is just over the horizon.

It is one thing to note the rise in importance of the media. It is another thing to explain it. Indeed, even in the Federalist and Jacksonian periods of the Republic, party newspapers were important for their communications function.

What is different in the late 20th Century is that the media seem to be on the verge of dominating political decision-making. As an example, President Carter got a good response to his July 15, 1979, energy message televised to the American public. But later that same week, when the President began a Cabinet shakeup following the verbal resignations of his Cabinet and senior staff, he immediately got bad reactions from the news media, and his short-term gains in public opinion polls were reversed. The Washington community--still viewing President Carter as an outsider--was hypercritical of this action. I can vouch for this because I was in Washington at the time and heard the news first-hand from Press Secretary Jody Powell at the time of a White House appointment.

An explanation of the rise in importance of the media can be developed by looking at population growth, which causes the American public to rely more heavily on the media. It also can be explained by technological advancements. It can be further explained by the vital role played by the media in reporting Vietnam and Watergate. Some media critics indeed have said the problem as we enter the 1980's is one if "media overkill"--that the media, which did not perform superlatively in the early days of Watergate--have been taking their watchdog role so seriously that when a rumor of Hamilton Jordan taking cocaine surfaces, they tend to rush into print with it. At this writing, in late 1979, some of the early testimony about these charges had been brought into doubt. Press Secretary Jody Powell had issued strong denials on several occasions.

Looking at the various reasons for the rise in importance of the media, one must take a close look at technological changes in communications. This is because the technological breakthroughs have expanded, many times over, the public's ability to follow major political events at the White House level. Indeed, the problem today may be more one of saturation with knowledge of or news about events than of a shortage of information. A critical need for interpretation exists today; this is where the current challenge to the media may lie. Programs like the MacNeil-Lehrer Report may be moving to meet this challenge--as well as others like the NBC White Papers, Bill Moyers' Journal, CBS Reports, and ABC Close-Up.

Technological changes in the 1980's and 1990's (in addition to fiberoptics and direct satellites) may include mural screen television, communication centers in the living room, two-way communications such as the QUBE **experiment** tried in Columbus and scheduled for further experimentation in Houston by Warner Communications. Our concern here is less with the technical side than with its political impact, however. The saturation with such political broadcasts may encourage unnecessary cynicism and feelings of powerlessness. Bill Moyers, Press Secretary under President Johnson in 1955 and 1956, said in a recent speech that Americans had moved from demonstrations and anger in the 1960's to resignation in the 1970's as a feeling of inability

to impact on events began to spread.[4] This may ᵇ
have been part of a leadership crisis in the West,ᵢ
however, as much as a situation of satiation.

Some of the political reaction to technological changes in communications has consisted of fear
on the part of political practitioners and the public that the media may be becoming too powerful.
A whole series of Supreme Court opinions during the
late 1970's have tended to put this belief in
doubt.[5]

So much for the context of the White House relationship between officials and correspondents.
It's time to move into the evolution of the relationship, in a quick-sketch fashion.

Early Forerunners of Press Aides--During the
19th Century, some Presidents did seek advice on
press relations. Pierre Salinger pointed out in a
personal interview that Nathaniel Hawthorne, the
author, performed this service for President Franklin Pierce (1853-1857).[6] This may be one of the
earliest instances of this kind of advice, but
Louis Koenig, leading presidential scholar, has described the work of aides who performed a press advice function along with other duties. Koenig
suggests that this was done as early in the 20th
Century as the Theodore Roosevelt Administration,
when Archie Butt was one of TR's principal advisers. This function was carried out later in the
20th Century Presidency by Joseph P. Tumulty, who

---

[4]Speech by Bill Moyers to University of Toledo
Friends of the Library, Inverness Club, Toledo, Ohio,
reported in Toledo Blade, September 27, 1979, and
delivered September 26.

[5]See Bruce W. Sanford, "No Quarter From This
Court", Columbia Journalism Review, September/
October 1979, pp. 59-63.

[6]Salinger interview, Paris, September 18,
1979.

handled President Wilson's media relations. The
differentiation of the Press Secretary function
finally became permanently established, some experts believe, at the time of the Franklin D.
Roosevelt Administration.[7]

Stephen T. Early and Ross McIntyre were charged
with media relations during the Roosevelt period,
but the function of press secretary was apparently
just becoming established.[8]

During President Truman's tenure, Press Secretaries included Charles Ross, long-time Washington correspondent for the St. Louis _Post-Dis-
patch_; Joseph Short, who succeeded Ross following
Ross's death, and finally Roger Tubby, who served
briefly.

All the media relations of the Roosevelt and
Truman periods predated nationwide television, although of course television was known in that time.
FDR visited the New York World's Fair in 1939 to
appear on experimental television, and Harry Truman
used TV in the late 1940's, but the real advent of
national television came with Truman's successor.

<u>Establishment of a Pattern in Media Relations</u>:
<u>James C. Hagerty</u>--Generally conceded to be some-

---

[7]See Louis W. Koenig, _The Invisible Presidency_
(New York: Rinehart, 1960). See also John Morton
Blum, _Joe Tumulty and the Wilson Era_ (Boston:
Houghton Mifflin, 1951), especially pp. 48, 51, 61-
65, and 171-173.

[8]A source at the Franklin D. Roosevelt Library indicated that Early styled himself Secretary
to the President and said that McIntyre carried the
actual title of Press Secretary. Visit to FDR Library, Hyde Park, New York, October 1977, under
sponsorship of Center for the Study of the Presidency.

thing of a genius at media relations, James C. Hagerty became Press Secretary for President Eisenhower at the time when television was just going nationwide. He began his work in January 1953 as a White House official, and Hagerty developed many practices which--with some modification--are still a part of White House media relations today.

Hagerty came from a background as a reporter for the New York _Times_ during an apprenticeship. He had come from a newspaper family (his father was a Washington correspondent in Theodore Roosevelt's era) and he worked in Albany as a statehouse correspondent after a period of apprenticeship in journalism. While in Albany, he was offered a position with Governor Thomas E. Dewey as press aide. The story is told that Hagerty told Dewey he was not one of his fondest admirers, and Dewey replied that this didn't make any difference because Hagerty was one of the best professionals to be found in Albany or anywhere. Up until 1952, Hagerty worked for Governor Dewey. Then he joined General Eisenhower during the 1952 campaign. He went to the White House with Eisenhower and served eight full years as Press Secretary. Eisenhower thought so highly of Hagerty that he sought his counsel even on matters going beyond press relations. Though there has been some controversy about this, Hagerty was extremely well organized, had a real skill in dealing with the media, and was effective the whole time--particularly during three occasions when Eisenhower had illnesses--a heart attack at Denver in 1955, an ileitis operation in Washington the following year, and a stroke in Washington in 1957. Hagerty definitely set the pattern for the modern White House media operation.

Functioning of _the_ _Modern_ _White_ _House_ _Press_ _Office_--Since Hagerty's time, the following persons have served as Press Secretary: Pierre Salinger for President Kennedy (and briefly for President Johnson); George E. Reedy, Bill Moyers and George Christian for President Johnson; Ron Ziegler and

Gerald Warren for President Nixon; Jerald terHorst
and Ron Nessen for President Ford, and Jody Powell
for President Carter.

During the period since Hagerty, two main
changes have occurred. These are enlargement of
the White House Press Office, and a reshuffling of
priorities in which network television gets top
billing over newspapers and wire services (although
the latter remain quite important).

At this point, I'll move to a description of
the White House Press Office personnel.

The present organization of the communications
function in the White House includes both a Communications Office and a Press Office.

Working in the Communications Office in the
Carter White House are the Assistant to the President for Communications, a Deputy Assistant working under the Assistant to the President, a Co-
ordinator of Communications, a five-member team of
speechwriters working under an Executive Speechwriter, a TV Co-ordinator, and a Media Advance
Director with a special assistant. The Assistant
to the President for Communications also has an
executive secretary, and his deputy has an administrative assistant.

Holding the Assistant to the President for
Communications post until his resignation in 1979
to join the Carter-Mondale 1980 campaign was Gerald
M. Rafshoon. After Rafshoon's departure, his deputy, Gregory S. Schneiders, became acting Assistant
to the President for Communications.

Working in the Press Office in the Carter
White House, in addition to the Press Secretary to
the President, are the Press Secretary's two executive assistants, a deputy Press Secretary (a second deputy's position is authorized but was vacant
in April 1979), two Associate Press Secretaries
with general responsibilities in addition to an

8

Associate Press Secretary working with the Office
of Media Liaison. There was also a News Summary
Editor and a Deputy Editor. In addition, a Photo-
graphic Office Director was serving, and a special
Press Release Office was in operation. The key
person in the operation in addition to Powell was
Rex L. Granum, the Deputy Press Secretary.

The fact that a staff of 10, while large when
compared to the Kennedy White House's small press
staff, still is much smaller than the Washington
correspondent corps accredited to the White House,
was pointed out by senior correspondent Frank
Cormier.[9]

The responsibilities of the White House Press
Office are mainly concerned with the function of
assisting the White House correspondent corps with
its task of covering the activities of the Presi-
dent--known inelegantly as "the body watch"-- and
the people working directly under him. The White
House embraces the President's personal staff, the
Executive Office of the President, and the various
agencies that are attached directly to the President, such as the National Security Council and
the Council of Economic Advisers.

Previous analyses of the White House Press
Office have been made with a focus solely on that
subject and as part of broader studies.

Elmer O. Cornwell Jr. made a study of the
public opinion function of the Presidency. Although
he traced the evolution of the media function,
his book concentrated on the years from Franklin D.
Roosevelt and Lyndon B. Johnson. It was a modern
classic and is still a very useful work. The high-
light of Cornwell's book was a case study of the
way in which Franklin D. Roosevelt "sold" the idea
of Social Security to the American public in the

---

[9]Interview with Frank Cormier, conducted by
telephone in Washington, July 1979.

1930's with an educational campaign which relied heavily on the press.[10]

Louis Koenig has written of the press aides to the President as part of a more general study of advisers.[11] Patrick Anderson has also written a study of White House advisers which includes material about modern Press Secretaries.[12]

Recent research funded with a Ford Foundation grant has been done by two scholars at Towson State College in Maryland, Michael Baruch Grossman and Martha Kumar. They have presented a paper entitled "Milton's Army" regarding the White House press corps, and they have published articles portraying their interpretation of the White House correspondent corps. They are co-authors of a major study which was to have appeared in 1980.[13]

Still another study which includes material on White House news operations, although it focuses more on the internal politics of the communications industry, is David Halberstam's monumental study of

---

[10]Elmer O. Cornwell Jr., Presidential Leadership of Public Opinion (Bloomington, Indiana: Indiana University Press, 1965). See especially Chapter 6, pp. 115-141.

[11]See Koenig, op. cit.

[12]See Patrick Anderson, The President's Men (Garden City, N.Y.: Doubleday Anchor Books, 1969). Anderson's book contains an especially good profile of Bill Moyers.

[13]Grossman and Kumar, "Milton's Army", Paper presented to Presidency Research Group, American Political Science Association annual meeting, Washington, August 1979; Grossman and Kumar, "The White House and the News Media", Political Science Quarterly Spring, 1979 (94: 1), pp. 37-53.

the American elite media. Halberstam has done
extensive interviewing with media figures in
management and executive positions, as well as
with press officials and with working correspondents.[14]

Doubtless there will be more and more studies,
including individual biographies of varied Press
Secretaries, as interest in this field continues.
James David Barber, a specialist in political
psychology, is currently at work on a follow-up
study of the media-government relationship which
is a continuation of his excellent study of campaign coverage by the media.

It remains to describe modern patterns of news
conferences. These have varied from the infrequent
news conferences of Richard Nixon to the relatively
frequent ones of Carter, Roosevelt and Truman.
Gerald Ford and John F. Kennedy had fairly frequent
ones.

Each President has sought news conference
formats which would be most congenial to him. Some
have reverted to the pencil-and-pad format of re-
ceiving reporters and correspondents in the Oval
Office. That was FDR's favorite type of news conference, with much banter and byplay. Harry Truman
did this also but in addition held news conferences
in the Indian Treaty Room of the Old State, War,
Navy Building (now known as the Old Executive Office
Building). Eisenhower often held news conferences
there; President Kennedy used the new State Department auditorium. Even though some correspondents
criticized his news conferences as "too theatrical",
it can scarcely be doubted that Kennedy--a former

---

[14]See David Halberstam, The Powers That Be
(New York: Random House, 1978). Halberstam does
an excellent job but he is not so harsh with media
heroes as he is in The Best and the Brightest
(Greenwich, Conn.: Fawcett Crest Books, 1972), a
book about the Vietnam era which covers JFK and LBJ.

11

reporter--used this approach quite skillfully. Lyndon Johnson experimented a great deal. He conducted East Room news conferences, walking news conferences on the South Lawn, conferences in the old EOB, and in other locations. Richard Nixon developed the idea of taking the news conference "out to the country". Gerald Ford did this on numerous occasions, and Jimmy Carter, while making use of the East Room, has in the latter half of his term tended to make more out-of-town appearances. (Even candidate Ronald Reagan held "citizen news conferences" in 1976.) The Carter relationship with the media, good at first, tended to turn somewhat sour in the final part of his term. Grossman and Kumar suggest that every President tends to go through cycles in news coverage--a buildup in which the media help the new President to get known, a period of antagonism in which the President is sometimes asked rather hostile, or at least probing questions, and a final period which amounts to a standoff.[15]

No doubt new Presidents will use the formats that seem most congenial to them for news conferences. But Presidential news conferences are not the only form of meeting with the press at the White House.

The other form such communication takes is that of a briefing for the news media correspondents held in the White House Press briefing room usually by the Press Secretary or by his principal aide. Jody Powell has been in the habit of holding one of these daily. In Salinger's time two a day were held. At this time the correspondents can follow up questions asked earlier, or post queries they may not have had an opportunity to ask the President at the regular news conferences. These briefings sometimes turned into snarling matches during Ziegler's tenure, but nonetheless they are quite useful. They not only help enlighten the

---

[15]Grossman and Kumar, Forthcoming Study.

correspondents, but they give the President an opportunity to use this forum to put emphasis on their views. Sometimes President Carter has visited the briefing room personally when he has had a particular point to make, but the briefing is peculiarly the mode of the Press Secretary in modern practice.

Thus one sees that the White House Press Office operation has evolved from an anonymous spokesman's occasional meeting with the press, into the modern operation, more highly structured and much more specialized. As Frank Cormier noted, the White House correspondent corps has grown far more than has the White House Press Office, but where Salinger in 1961-1963 could operate with a handful of people the operation is noticeably larger now.

After this introduction I'll move next to analysis of the specific Press Secretaries and the very different modes of operation. The analysis will begin with a look at Hagerty's and Salinger's operations as press secretary.

Acme/United Press International
Courtesy, Herbert Hoover Library

George Akerson was the first officially appointed White House Press
Secretary. Here he and President Hoover with military officers stand
at the Chilean-Argentine frontier in 1929.

Courtesy, Franklin D. Roosevelt Library

Franklin D. Roosevelt, Stephen Early (center) and Winston Churchill at the
Yalta Conference in 1945.

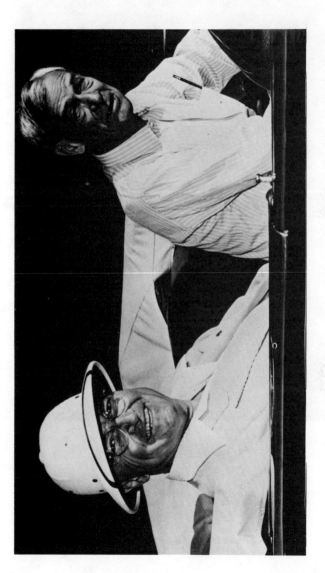

U. S. Navy Photograph
Courtesy, Harry S Truman Library

Charlie Ross served as President Truman's first Press Secretary until
Ross's untimely death in 1949. The two are shown here at Key West, Fla.

Truman and his second Press Secretary, Joe Short,
take a morning walk at Key West, Fla.

Roger Tubby served as President Truman's third
and last Press Secretary.

CHAPTER TWO

PRESS SECRETARIES AND THEIR VIEW OF THE OFFICE (I):

JAMES C. HAGERTY AND PIERRE SALINGER

Hagerty's Role in Establishing the Modern Operation for News Dissemination--As indicated in the
brief summary in Chapter One, the modern White
House news dissemination operation really dates
from James C. Hagerty, President Eisenhower's Press
Secretary from 1953 to 1961.

Mr. Hagerty kept a remarkable diary for more
than a year of his tenure as Press Secretary during President Eisenhower's first term.

This diary gives an excellent insight into the
nature of the operation of the White House Press
Office and the duties of the Press Secretary.

Matters covered in the Hagerty Diaries included a description of the day of President
Eisenhower's heart attack in September 1955, plus
an indication of the kinds of contacts Hagerty was
constantly making on the President's behalf with
network executives, newspaper publishers and party
notables.[1]

Segments of the Hagerty Diary disclosed dis-
cussions of the following matters on the days indicated:

Wednesday, December 8, 1954--Press conference

---

[1]For quotations about the Eisenhower heart
attack, see William C. Spragens, The Presidency and
the Mass Media in the Age of Television (Washington:
University Press of America, 1978), pp. 325-334.

agenda discussed at 8:30 a.m. staff conference included briefing with opening statements on the
"Atoms for Peace" plan, Senator Joseph McCarthy,
meeting with congressional Republican leaders,
Secretary Mitchell's speech on labor policy, the
Eisenhower legislative program, foreign policy
matters including Secretary Dulles and the Big
Four foreign ministers conference, and Chip Bohlen
controversy (ambassador).

Following the staff meeting a conversation
with Allen Dulles and a pre-news conference briefing with Secretary of State John Foster Dulles
were related. The latter dealt with: "Atoms for
Peace"; U.N. resolution on American fliers held by
the Chinese government; French Prime Minister
Mendes-France's proposal for a meeting with the
Soviet Union; resignation of Japanese Premier
Yoshida; report from Ambassador "Chip" Bohlen;
comments on West German elections.

A discussion with President Eisenhower and a
later talk with correspondents are related in these
excerpts:

"I went over my notes with him (President
Eisenhower), saving the McCarthy matter for last.
On that he said, 'You don't have to coach me on
this one, Jim. I have been giving some thought to
it overnight and I am merely going to say that I
am not going to indulge in vituperation. I hope
they ask me questions about the role I believe the
Republican Party must take in the future, and I'm
going to give them quite a talk on progressive
moderates.'

"The President was quite insistent that he
handle this in his own way and when Jerry Morgan
and Jerry Persons started to interrupt to suggest
something, he leaned across his desk and said,
'Listen, my boys, I'm glad this happened. I can
never work with this fellow and I never thought I
could. You asked me to try it and I did. But I'm
glad the break has come because as far as I'm concerned, this fellow isn't ever going to get into

16

the White House anymore and don't any of you ever come with a proposal that he does. The McCarthys, the Jenners, the Brickers and the rest of them can do what they want as far as I'm concerned, but I'm going to do one thing. I'm going to get this Republican Party of ours to be progressive or else-- and that's that!'. . .

"Walking across the street to the press conference, Murray Snyder gave the President a beautiful line which he used quite effectively to the effect that the new Democratic National Chairman reminded him of a politician who spent all his time looking into a looking glass instead of out the window. At the end of the press conference the President got quite a chuckle out of the reactions to this remark and said, 'I used it in connection with the question on Butler, by saying also "that some politician who looking into the glass sees only reflections of doubt and fear and the kind of confusion that he often tries to create" I was referring to a lot more people than Butler and I hope the newsmen realize that.'

* * * * *

"After the conference I talked to a few of the reporters--including Smitty (Merriman Smith, United Press International), Marv Arrowsmith (Associated Press), Roscoe Drummond (syndicated columnist), and Eddie Folliard (Washington _Post_)--and told them that I thought there was a good political story in the conference. The President's use of the words, 'progressive moderates', his insistence that any future nominee of the party reflect those views, and his turndown of McCarthy with the expression that if the Right Wing wanted to leave the party, that was their business--was a pretty good blueprint of the President's political thinking. They agreed with this, and all wrote separate stories to that effect."

The entry for Tuesday, July 27, 1954, summarized Hagerty's conversation with the President regarding Syngman Rhee of South Korea in the second

floor living quarters. Other topics discussed included the President's visit to Denver, Hagerty's
work, the 1956 re-election campaign, and pressures
of office. This excerpt refers to the last two
items:

"3. 1956--For the first time the President
virtually told me that he would run again in '56.
He put it this way: 'A lot of people are urging
me to run again for another term. They say that
I should never discuss this or give any indication
of which way I'm going to decide until the very
last moment in 1956. I suppose they're right.
But when the time comes to make this decision, I
will make it by myself after consultation with a
few people in the White House, including yourself,
Jerry Persons and Sherm Adams. Right now I kind
of think that the answer will be that I will run
for another term, but I am telling everyone that
they better not speculate on this and let me make
the decision. After all, it is my life and it
will have to be my decision.'

4. "Tension--The President told me that he
was beginning for the first time to feel the ten-
sion of his office. He thought that was only
natural because of the closing weeks of the Congressional session plus the very heavy burden of
international decisions which he has had to make
these days. 'It's not the job particularly that
bothers me or the title. It's the multiplicity
of petty problems that people bring to me. The
selfishness of the members of Congress is incred-
ible and the manner in which they try to put me
on the spot and want me to decide questions that
never should be brought to me are just about
driving me nuts.' The President said that he was
trying to get away this weekend to Camp David. .
. . The legislative leaders meeting has been
postponed until Tuesday morning and he was sure
that if he could get three complete days away
from the job, he would feel a lot better. . . .
Why he hasn't blown his top before this is something I'll never understand."

The remaining quotations are from entries
for March 25 and March 28, 1955:

Friday, March 25, 1955

". . .The only thing of note today is that I
got the White House off the hook on the squirrels.

"I talked to the President in the morning and
told him that I thought we had better once and for
all kill the squirrel story by saying that three
squirrels were trapped and removed from the White
House grounds, but the situation seemed to have
cleared up and the putting green was no longer
being dug up by our furry little friends. He
laughed and said that he agreed with me so at my
10:30 press conference, I told the newsmen that I
had been hearing a great deal of talk about squirrels lately and that actually the facts were these:
That the President had noticed that the squirrels
were digging up the putting green, which was given
to the White House by the United States Golf Association. He had mentioned it to the people in the
White House and action had been taken to try to
correct it. Three squirrels were trapped, two of
which were shipped to Rock Creek Park and one to
Virginia. I said that I have not yet been able to
find out why that one went to Virginia, but I supposed one of the gardeners just took it out there
one evening. I told the newsmen that I had had no
kicks from the squirrels that they did not like
their new domiciles, and this cleared up the story
as far as the putting green was concerned.

"I naturally took a lot of kidding on this in
the stories that followed, but it had the effect
I wanted--it ended the squirrel controversy."[2]

─────────

[2]President Carter in mid-summer 1979 had a
similar problem with animals. His problem concerned a "killer rabbit" seen in a Georgia swamp
while the President was out canoeing alone.

". . . Had Bill Lawrence of the New York
Times in today to raise hell about a _Times_ Review
of the Week piece last Sunday which said among
other things that 'anger by the Democrats over the
release of the Yalta papers was a result of the
way the Department (meaning the State Department)
a day before giving the text to the _Times_ had
tried to send confidential copies to Senator George
and others on the Hill.' I told Lawrence that I
thought this was one hell of a way to run a rail-
road and that to this day I did not know how they
got their report, but if they did get it from the
State Department and publicly admitted it, that
was one sure way of not getting anything in the
future.

"Bill was actually flabbergasted to read the
Review of the Week piece and he called Scotty Reston immediately. Reston had been away for the
weekend and had not seen the article and was as
amazed at it as Bill. Lawrence said he had called
Sulzberger directly and Sulzberger had Lester
Merkel, the editor of the Sunday _Times_, call him
back. Merkel said that it was just a mistake and
that it had slipped through. I am sure that both
Reston and Lawrence are telling me the truth on
this and that it was an error.

"We agreed we should not do anything about
it now, but I warned both Reston and Lawrence that
if the issue was raised in Congress, we would have
to deny it and that I fully expected them to deny
it also. They agreed to do so."[3]

James Hagerty had a fine relationship with
President Eisenhower and his staff associates,

---

[3]Material quoted from the James C. Hagerty
Diaries, compiled in 1977 during a visit to the
Dwight D. Eisenhower Library, Abilene, Kansas,
and used with Mr. Hagerty's permission.

from all accounts of that period of White House
history.[4]

The period of the Hagerty tenure in the White
House Press Office was one in which Hagerty had
developed a well-organized press operation, and
his outgoing manner of dealing with people was
quite useful to President Eisenhower, who perhaps
because of his military background had the reputation in the correspondent corps (by most accounts)
of being friendly but a bit aloof.

One important point was made by Mr. Hagerty
himself at a Center for the Study of the Presidency Symposium at Montauk in 1970 when the former Press Secretary said:

> One of the arguments that I have
> with some people, including the news media,
> is that it is completely ridiculous to try
> to compare one Presidential term or one
> President, with another. Situations change.
> Problems change.
>
> Let's take the Administration I was
> associated with. After President Eisenhower
> made a settlement regarding Korea, there

---

[4]See, for example, references to Hagerty and
the media in Merriman Smith, Meet Mr. Eisenhower
(New York: Harper and Brothers, 1955), pp. 11-13,
100-101, 215; Sherman Adams, First-Hand Report:
The Story of the Eisenhower Administration (New
York: Harper & Brothers, 1961), pp. 39, 53-54, 72,
74, 80, 84, 95-96, 119, 137, 142, 147, 166, 188,
190, 194, 198, 214, 225, 228-229, 234, 285, 292,
294, 349, 352, 355, 357-358, 391, 445, 448;
Robert J. Donovan, Eisenhower: The Inside Story
(New York: Harper & Brothers, 1956), pp. 20, 40,
201, 248, 251, 278, 308, 321, 366-368, 378, 394
ff., 403; Merlo J. Pusey, Eisenhower the President
(New York: Macmillan, 1956), pp. 26, 33, 89, 91,
93, 116.

was no place in this world where we had
the international problems which the Administrations have been involved in from
1961 on. The same thing was true of domestic problems. Our major . . . MAJOR .
. . . civil rights confrontation was
Little Rock. And Little Rock seems to
be way in the past and rather minute
compared to a Watts, to a Newark and other
confrontations you have at the present
time.

So each President determines the tone
and the policies of his Administration.
He is the indisputable leader of his Administration. . . . I did nothing except what
my boss told me to do--and say. . . .[5]

The various evidence indicates that Mr. Hagerty was a thorough-going professional who on occasion
took "trouble-shooting" assignments from President
Eisenhower. From his own testimony, it would appear that President Eisenhower was very much in
command of his own administration, contrary to
what some media reports at the time indicated.
Perhaps the closest parallel to what Mr. Hagerty
did in his time may be found--despite Hagerty's
warning not to make comparisons across time and
across Administrations--in Jody Powell, President
Carter's Press Secretary.

Evidence seen by the author during a 1977
visit to the Dwight D. Eisenhower Library in
Abilene, Kansas, indicates that Hagerty was invited to stag functions at the White House and
that he attended on a regular basis. However, the
author's own observation in Washington and in research on the White House environment has been that
there is normally a clearly drawn dichotomy between official and social life of most Presidents.

---

[5]R. Gordon Hoxie, ed., The White House: Organization and Operations (Proceedings of the 1970
Montauk Symposium) (New York: Center for the Study
of the Presidency, 1971), pp. 53-54.

For all the parties thrown for the press by FDR, and for all the warmth of the relationship between President Kennedy and the news media, this dichotomy has been largely preserved. If one reflects on the nature of official relationships in Washington, this dichotomy is understandable and is at least to some degree logical. A great deal is at stake, and the persons near or at the power center need some time in which they can feel they are able to relax. This is difficult to do in the presence of official associates. Thus the tradition of the Kitchen Cabinet (Jackson), the Tennis Cabinet (Coolidge), and in more modern times the association of Presidents with major donors and benefactors. This is merely another way of saying that despite our professions American society is not totally egalitarian--and when dealing with Presidents we realistically might not expect it to be totally so. Thus, there tend to be peer groups, the President and his pre-election friends, the upper echelon staff, the middle and lower echelon staff, and "in-and-outers" (experts from various fields working temporarily in Washington but expecting to return to home base).

As for James Hagerty's relationship with the news media of the 1950's, two statements are necessary. The first is that the great majority of news professionals respected and admired Hagerty's own professionalism, and his flair for dealing with the media. His Irish wit, and his ability to remove tensions from a potentially tense situation, stood him in good stead.[6]

Although it became fashionable during the Nixon-Agnew period (1969-1973) to speak of the re-

---

[6]This author recalls such a situation at the Fifth Annual National Leadership Symposium of the Center for the Study of the Presidency at Nashville in October 1973. A political scientist asked a pointed question about Don Nixon at a time when impeachment talk was in the air. Hagerty deflated a potentially touchy situation with a witty remark. And it was perfectly natural.

lationship between the White House and the news
media as an "adversary relationship", and there
is some of this in it, I've always contended that
it's just as much of a symbiotic relationship, in
which each partner depends on the other. News media depend on public officials for information, and
public officials depend on the media for a part in
image-building with the public. I think this is a
more appropriate kind of model for Press Secretaries to strive for, and I think Hagerty was usually
very able in doing this.

During the 1950's, television was beginning to
come into its own. The wire services and elite
newspapers such as the Washington Post and New York
Times did tend to dominate the relationship, but
the viewership of television was growing rapidly.
Hagerty made an effort to accommodate this by permitting filming of the President's "press conferences" by the then-available film and kinescope
processes. The film and kinescope was reviewed by
the White House Press Office, apparently under the
instructions of the President, and the most significant parts of it were released for use by the
media. Actualities (recorded voices for radio)
were just then coming into more general use, and
these made coverage more realistic. Also the technology was taking great strides, and Hagerty wanted
to keep up with it in order to permit the President
to be seen to the best advantage, but still within
the context of an open society's news coverage
(both critical and complimentary).

So Hagerty had a good relationship with the
news media of the 1950's. The media were more
trusting in those days than now; this pre-Watergate
condition lasted until perhaps 1964 for the most
part. Respect for the Presidency still exists today, but there is now a feeling that it must be
earned by the incumbent. In that somewhat more
innocent day, it was often accorded almost automatically as a kind of byproduct of patriotism.

Hagerty was responsible for systematizing the
briefing system at the White House, when it was ne-

cessary to follow up news conference remarks by
the President.

In general, it can be said that Hagerty really
set the tone of the modern White House Press Office.
Growth has occurred, and refinements have been added. But the lineaments or outlines of the basic
media operation remain remarkably similar to what
they were in the Eisenhower-Hagerty period of White
House media relations.

<u>Salinger's Role in Further Developing the
Modern Press Office Function</u>--The evolution of
technology in the Press Office did not end with
Hagerty's tenure there. It was followed up in the
John F. Kennedy Administration by the very able
Pierre Salinger. As Mr. Salinger noted in a Paris
interview with this author, "President Kennedy
could have been his own Press Secretary if he had
had the time."[7] Mr. Salinger also noted that President Kennedy had himself had experience as a member of the working press as a reporter (he covered
the San Francisco founding conference of the United
Nations, as mentioned in biographical writings of
James MacGregor Burns and Joan and Clay Blair Jr.[8])

It has been written in various places that had
President Kennedy lived, he would have sought a
post-White House career as a newspaper publisher or
perhaps a University lecturer. (He would have been

---

[7]Personal interview with Pierre Salinger, Press
Secretary for the late President Kennedy, in ABC
News Bureau, 22 Avenue d'Eylau, Paris, September
18, 1979.

[8]See Joan and Clay Blair Jr., <u>The Search for
JFK</u> (New York: Berkley/G.P. Putnam's Sons, 1976),
Chapter 27, "The Journalist", pp. 371-388, especial-
ly pp. 371-379; also see James MacGregor Burns,
<u>John Kennedy: A Political Profile</u> (New York: Avon
Book Division of Hearst Corp., 1960), pp. 67-68.

51 at retirement.)

As for technological changes during the Kennedy-Salinger period in the White House, Salinger moved from the edited version of the President's news conferences to live coverage of President Kennedy's news conferences. Despite some critics' description of these news conferences as theatrical (a running debate on whether quick recall and command of facts are as crucial and important as decision-making poise still continues), it can scarcely be doubted that the Kennedy news conferences were almost _sui generis_. Franklin D. Roosevelt was a master of the media but in his era he lacked television, being obliged to work only with radio. John F. Kennedy was the first President to realize and actualize the full potential of television for a Chief Executive. His shrewd judgement caused him to question whether overexposure was possible, and he did attempt to limit the frequency of White House news conferences, and also the frequency of direct telecasts to the public (such as he used during the 1962 Cuban missile crisis).

By this time, the rise of television was apparent to all, but it was still several years before television began to become the dominant medium in news coverage for the general public. (The shift from 15-minute to 30-minute evening newscasts by the major commercial networks is one of the symbolic landmarks of this era).

The Kennedy news conferences were held at the new State Department Auditorium in Foggy Bottom. They were a show that all of Washington enjoyed. The author spoke in late 1978 with a former Republican member of Congress, who talked of how Kennedy's popularity on the Hill caused some congressman to go over and observe JFK's news conferences. (Without reflecting on Kennedy's successors, it is difficult to imagine congressman of 1979 or 1980 going all the way to the State Department to observe the President conducting a news conference, but of course President Kennedy had a reputation as a virtuoso of this media format.)

26

Live television news conferences, then, are a
contribution of JFK and Salinger. In addition to
this, President Kennedy (as an outgrowth of the
1960 campaign against Richard Nixon) had developed
a system for having himself briefed before meeting
the media correspondents.[9]

Briefing books are a routine of campaign and
news conference appearances by modern Presidents,
but the practice in its modern form was systemat-
ized in Salinger's era in the Press Office, even
though similar practices were used by JFK's predecessors, notably Eisenhower with the aid of
Hagerty.

In addition to the pre-briefing given the
President, a system was developed (quite popular
with the correspondent corps) of two-a-day briefings for the media, usually handled by the Press
Secretary or one of his senior deputies. The
Deputy Press Secretary could handle such matters
in the Kennedy era in the absence of the Press Secretary. Some delegation of release of routine
news might occur, but the principal aim of the
briefing appeared to be clarification and greater
depth of information presented to the news media.
The two-a-day practice, according to both Salinger
and Frank Cormier, has now been replaced by a sort
of "floating" one-a-day system. This has also
been confirmed by Bob Schieffer, a former White
House correspondent for CBS, and Robert Pierpoint
who remains a CBS White House correspondent.[10]

---

[9]The September-October 1979 issue of Washington Journalism Review discusses how counter-brief-
ing sessions are now being held by the media to
discuss coordinating of questioning of the President. However, I have found no evidence in printed or original sources of this practice being done
on a common or organized basis during the Kennedy
era.

[10]Information derived from a personal interview
with Schieffer, at the White House, December 18,
1978, and from a telephone interview with Pierpoint,
August 6, 1979.

Mr. Salinger is currently an active European correspondent for ABC News based in Paris.[11] In this capacity, this noted newsman has prepared series for ABC on the Irish Republican Army, and he has given coverage to the visit of Pope John Paul II to Ireland in September 1979. But our principal concern with his career is his service as Press Secretary under President Kennedy from 1961 to 1963.

The following information[12] was all obtained from a personal interview with Mr. Salinger:

Salinger had worked for Robert Kennedy as his aide when he (RFK) was chief investigator for the Senate Labor Rackets Committee. Previous experience of Salinger dated to a local election in 1946 and the 1952 and 1956 presidential campaigns of Adlai Stevenson. In May or June of 1959, Senator (John F.) Kennedy, who was a member of the Senate Labor Rackets Committee, asked Salinger if he would start to work in September. Kennedy told Salinger he would be in charge of press relations. Salinger said, "So it came through my association with Robert Kennedy and of course John Kennedy, who was a member of the committee."

Salinger stressed the importance of "extensive" journalistic experience in acting effectively in the post of Press Secretary. He commented, "At the time I went to work for President Kennedy I'd had 14 years experience as a working journalist on the newspaper in San Francisco, the Chronicle, for a national magazine, Collier's magazine, and I think that experience was probably the most helpful

---

[11]He was one of those questioned following a Belfast IRA raid September 4, 1979. Toledo Blade, September 5, 1979, p. 3.

[12]The interview was conducted on the morning of September 18, 1979, at the Paris ABC Bureau, 22 Avenue d'Eylau, Paris.

of anything I'd had. Then, the second thing that
qualified me was having had the experience of having gone through the campaign of Senator Kennedy. .
. ."

The JFK campaign for the Presidency began with
travels in September 1959. As Salinger noted, "We
would take a few reporters with us and gradually
the number of reporters would increase until the
day of the election we had 500 reporters covering
our election headquarters in Hyannis Port, and then
the rise of the press interest in the campaign came
at the same time that I had a gradual (learning experience) and gained in my own knowledge of how to
handle the job and to be competent in it."

The political socialization and background of
press secretaries is something one would expect to
diffuse political values into future holders of
this office. This appeared to be true in Salinger's
case as he said of his early years:

I was brought up in a kind of a po -
litical family, that was vitally interested
in politics. . . . They weren't politicians
but they were interested in the issues of
their time and we talked politics around
the table.

And I remember from a very young age
that I was fascinated by politics and that's
why when I got out of the Navy in 1946 I
wanted to do something in the field of politics.

I worked in the campaign for Mayor of
San Francisco, and was involved in it off
and on then until I worked (in the campaign
of) 1960. I was very interested in it.

We were also a family that was a very
Democratic family, so I grew up in an atmos-
phere of Democratic thought, support for the
Democratic Party."

Questioned about his actual title while working for President Kennedy, Salinger noted, "I had the title of Press Secretary. That was the way my commission read (when I was appointed)." The present styling of the title is Press Secretary to the President.

Salinger described the workings of the White House Press Office during his tenure as Press Secretary. This is his recollection of the work done there during the Kennedy era:

"It did vary a lot. I had one principal assistant, who was an Associate White House Press Secretary, who was Andrew Hatcher. He was a Black journalist that I had known in San Francisco, and who had been in political campaigns with me almost since the start of my own political interest, and who I brought into the campaign during the 1959-1960 period. He stayed on with me at the White House. Then I created the post of Assistant Press Secretary, with the principal task of dealing with the foreign press. That job was held by two different men during the time at the White House. The first was named Jay Gildner, who I hired out of the USIA (United States Information Agency). He left me and went back to the USIA, and Malcolm Kilduff who I hired from the State Department. Those two men held that post during the time I was at the White House. Then we had five other people in the office; ladies who handled various responsibilities, (such as) secretarial (and supervising the) photographers--a very, very small office compared to what it is today. It's staggering, the White House Press Office is (now), and ours was very, very small."

Mr. Salinger stated that he talked to President Kennedy about either media matters or matters that might draw coverage on the average "five or six times a day". He explained that he and the President would be talking about "subjects in the news, subjects on which I was being questioned and I had frequent and open access to the President's office and saw him whenever I needed to.

I didn't need permission to go see him; I could just walk into his office and deal with him. And since I held in those days just two press conferences (or briefings) a day, I always had to see him just before each of the press conferences, so that I could get answers on questions I thought I was going to be asked. The press could ask questions on any subject they wanted to. The access was very, very open. In fact, that's the way the Kennedy White House worked. Certainly there were eight of us who had specific responsibilities inside the White House. There was no chief of staff, and each of seven or eight people had direct access to the President on a need basis."

Asked about the good and bad points in President Kennedy's relations with the news media, Mr. Salinger replied:

"I thought they were largely positive. First of all, John Kennedy had been a newspaperman, and probably more than any President I've observed had a fundamental knowledge of what the relationship should be between press and government. He could have been Press Secretary himself with no problem; he just didn't have the time. And he believed that the relationship should be open and as direct as possible; I can't think of any really negative side of his relation with the press. I mean he got angry with the press from time to time, but I think any President has some problems with the press. But he took a keen interest in what was said about him, as I think any President does.

"He was very accessible, and he would see newspapermen on an individual basis, perhaps several a day at the White House, at least one. I think the problem was that after the death of President Kennedy. . . he was replaced immediately by two Presidents, Lyndon Johnson and Richard Nixon, who did not understand what the central relationship was between government and the press. Both of whom believed that the press's responsibility was to become an arm of government, for patriotic reasons,

31

which if anybody would read the Constitution, they'd understand the debates that led up to the First Amendment just about abolished that idea."

When Salinger was asked to rate his predecessors in the job, he responded:

"I think of all the predecessors in the job, the one that was clearly the best, and I feel in my opinion the best Press Secretary that ever served in the White House, was James Hagerty. Hagerty worked for a President who didn't understand anything about the press; he took on that assignment. He was really the brains of the press operation; he was a professional, he was an able man. And I would rate him the highest of the people who served in that position. I think that if you study the past and the people who served as Press Secretary, you would also have to say that Stephen Early was also an exceedingly able man, in a different context though because in communications, as things changed in the years between Early and Hagerty-- Hagerty was really the first one who had to tackle the problem of television. Although we ended up having to tackle it when television was really coming into its own."

Salinger was asked to comment on the differences in function served by wire services correspondents, network correspondents, and correspondents for major and minor newspapers. He responded:

"The question is a good, legitimate question. And I think whether we want it or not, there is a hierarchy in coverage of the White House, and the Press Secretary is conscious of that hierarchy to the extent that he's aware of the need to get his President's message across to the broadest level of people. When I say television came into its own when I came into the White House in January of 1961, maybe not to the extent that it is today. But the television correspondent became bigger during the period when I was in the White House than he had been in the period before. For example, critical pools on presidential trips had not included tel-

evision. Television was included for the first
time in pools during the Kennedy Administration,
and it was the beginning of their power. The hierarchy that I found was the wire services, Number
One, with a large number of people, and then the
newspapers like the New York *Times* and the news-
magazines, *Newsweek* and the *U.S. News and World
Report*. The major newspapers and then was the
TV networks.

"Take today, and the intervening period between 1961 and now, the hierarchy has become even
more pronounced in that the networks dominate. At
the White House, that explains why the Press Secretary has a different mix as far as personnel today, and that explains why there is inside the White
House today a special section absorbed only with
television, because television has taken on great
import for what goes on at the White House. A
special section that deals strictly with television."

Salinger was also asked whether he found
governmental news different in dealing with the
media than was the case with campaign news. He replied:

"Not really. I think the difference is not in
governmental news as a generalized subject but in
some aspects of governmental news. Matters affect-
ing the national security of the nation--those
matters are obviously more difficult matters to
handle than those that come up in the campaign or
those in the normal course of business. And of
course a number of events rise that require very,
very special handling. One evident one was the
Cuban missile crisis of 1962, which went on during
a period when there was a real risk of nuclear war
for the United States. This was the toughest kind
of situation to handle, from the standpoint of information. But if you take the national security
element out, the handling of government news is not
any more difficult than that in the campaign."

I asked Salinger who among the Presidents other than President Kennedy had in his opinion the

best media relations and why. His views:

"I would say of modern Presidents, Roosevelt Number One. He was an absolute master of dealing with the press. I would say Truman. When you think that the concept of dealing with the press on an organized basis really only goes back to Wilson, although Nathaniel Hawthorne acted as a press adviser for President Franklin Pierce, the actual functional idea of having someone as a Press Secretary goes back to the days of Wilson. None of his successors up to Roosevelt was particularly good with the press--Harding, Hoover, Coolidge. I would say Roosevelt was the modern time master. Few were in his class, and then I would say the two worst were Johnson and Nixon. And Eisenhower, while not a genius at it, had what I would call a satisfactory relationship--mainly because of the talents of Hagerty."

Salinger was asked to elaborate on his view of his predecessors as Press Secretary. He noted that he had already referred to Hagerty and then he con- tinued:

". . . I think Hagerty was the best; Early was extremely competent. I knew briefly Joe Short and Charlie Ross, but not well enough to be the judge of what he (Short) did, and I did know Roger Tubby, who ended up as Truman's Press Secretary because he later worked for me in the Kennedy cam- paign. And he was a very efficient and fine Press Secretary, I would say. I think of the others prob- ably the best was Moyers. Reedy had an impossible job; he was a very competent man, (who served) later with Johnson. If you were able to ask Johnson to speak out of the grave, he would probably say George Christian. Because George Christian, of all the Press Secretaries he (LBJ) had, was the one who most faithfully did reflect Johnson's line. I think that under a situation that was an extremely difficult one, . . . Jody Powell has been an ex- cellent Press Secretary. . . . And I'd rather not comment on the rest of them."

Salinger was asked what kind of experience he
would recommend for Press Secretaries in the future.
His reply:

"Again I think it's got to be media experience.
And I think now that the television medium has become so powerful, I would think that the Press
Secretary should come out of television. The best
would be of course if he came out of both--if he
had a combination of being in the printed media
and television. If the choice were between the
two, I'd say, get a man out of television."

As a member of the Kennedy staff, Salinger re-
marked--as did Arthur Schlesinger Jr. and Myer
Feldman in separate interviews--that President
Kennedy had a great skill at promoting smooth
working relationships, with the use of humor and
informality.

Regarding working with President Kennedy,
Salinger said: "I was very comfortable working
with him. He had a way of putting people who
worked with him at ease; when I would have my first
meeting with him, there wasn't just serious talk.
At the beginning we would joke and gossip about
things that were happening and you felt totally
comfortable about President Kennedy. You weren't
in awe of him, and you didn't feel restrained. He
was a man who encouraged people who worked for him
to give their ideas and even disagree with him.
The only thing being that once a decision was
taken, you were expected to accept the decision.
And as long as I had input into the decision, I
didn't mind that."

Asked for a summary of changes in the White
House Press Office in the 1960's and 1970's, and
their implications, Salinger commented:

"I think the most obvious thing is that the
Press Office has undergone the most critical
changes in the last ten years; it's no longer the
same kind of place. And the two elements that were
most involved in that were the war in Vietnam and

Watergate. And today there exists a state of hostility between the press and the government that didn't exist in my day. And it's complicated enormously this relationship. I pity anybody that has to take that job (the job of Press Secretary) today."

In 1966, at the time he wrote his book about his service in the White House, Pierre Salinger stated:

"I believe that in one critical area of the relationship between the press and the government, . . . communications have broken down. This is the area of how the government and the press work with each other in the time of national crisis short of a declared war.

"We saw the problem at the time of the invasion of the Bay of Pigs, in the Cuban missile crisis of 1962, in the continuing struggle between the two institutions over information on the war in Vietnam.

"What is needed now is an honest effort to come to grips with this problem. I would suggest an immediate conference, away from Washington, in a setting which would induce informal but incisive discussion of this subject. The participants at this conference should be the top news executives of our major networks and wire services, the editors of a half dozen to a dozen leading newspapers, and the top people in the government entrusted with the responsibility of information. Perhaps the Aspen Institute for Humanistic Studies, in Aspen, Colorado, would lend its splendid facilities for such a meeting. . . . The central subject should be the dissemination of information by the government in the gray area of national security where the vital interests of our nation are at stake. . . ."[13]

---

[13]Pierre Salinger, <u>With Kennedy</u> (Garden City, N.Y.: Doubleday & Co., 1966), p. 368.

At a symposium at Gonzaga University in Washington State in April 1978, Mr. Salinger discussed some of the national security problems of the White House Press Office in the company of other former Press Secretaries. One of the points made in the discussion was that appointed officials such as Press Secretaries and elected officials such as Presidents are responsible for the security of more than 200 million Americans, while journalists are not. At this same meeting, another participant suggested that no journalist could understand the problem who had never worked at the White House, and Seymour Hersh of the New York _Times_ immediately attacked this statement.

At the Gonzaga Symposium, Salinger described Press Secretaries as "not very important people". He emphasized that they are always responsible to the Presidents whom they serve; he saw them as playing a quite secondary role. As indicated in the Paris interview, he felt he was doing things for the President in media relations that the President would have been quite capable of doing for himself except that he lacked the time.

Salinger suggested at Gonzaga that there is more hostility toward press secretaries at present than when he served in the White House. He did not claim that the Kennedy Administration was error free and described some difficulties he encountered at the time of the 1962 Cuban missile crisis. He indicated that the Kennedy Administration talked openly about Vietnam, and also that it had a much smaller operation--comparatively speaking--than is true of the White House Press Office today.[14]

Transition in the Press Office (1953-1963)--
In the period between the opening of the Eisenhower Administration in 1953 and the Kennedy Assassination

---

[14]The _Presidential Press Secretaries' Forum,_ _April 1, 1978, Campus of Gonzaga University,_ pp. 3, 4, 6, 9, 10, 11.

in 1963, major changes took place in the fabric of
the media-government relationship as reflected in
the vortex of the White House Press Office. The
nation was fortunate in that it was served at that ime
and its Presidents were served, by two very able
Press Secretaries. Each in his own way contributed
to the development of the modern Press Office, and
each helped to share what it is today, but the maj-
or contribution was doubtless that of Hagerty;
both men have been praised by other press secretaries.

Courtesy, Dwight D. Eisenhower Library

James C. Hagerty of the Eisenhower staff is considered the Press Secretary who contributed most to the modern office.

Courtesy, John F. Kennedy Library

Pierre Salinger, now ABC Bureau Chief in Paris and a former writer for L'Express and U. S. Senator, introduced live television coverage of White House news conferences for President John F. Kennedy. Here the two men confer during a 1962 congressional campaign tour.

PRESS SECRETARIES AND THEIR VIEW OF THE OFFICE (II):

LYNDON JOHNSON'S PRESS OFFICE

Lyndon Johnson's Press Secretaries--Not count-
ing Pierre Salinger, who served for a few months
as a holdover from the Kennedy Administration,
President Lyndon Johnson had three Press Secretaries during slightly more than five years in
the White House. President Johnson, who had
tremendous drive from all reports, was a difficult man to work for. He could be a slavedriver,
but he could also be compassionate. Reports from
his associates indicate that he had an ingratiat-
ing manner even when he had scourged or reprimand-
ed a subordinate. This trait or characteristic
may explain in part the turnover in the Press Office under President Johnson. The rest of the
explanation may lie in the technological explo-
sion that was beginning in that time--color TV,
microwave relay advances, experimental work with
satellites, and the like.

At any rate, the three men who served Lyndon
Johnson as Press Secretary included the immensely
talented George E. Reedy, a scholarship winner at
the University of Chicago (in Latin, English and
History) in the early days of Robert M. Hutchins'
"New Plan"[1] and a long-time member of the Johnson

---

[1]President Johnson heard a reference to Mr.
Reedy as "one of Hutchins' whiz kids" (an epithet
applied to many Chicago graduates in the '30's) and
assumed it was a reference to the children on the
airwaves--radio "quiz kids" program. Reedy said he
was "never able to scotch the story as Johnson
liked it so much that he kept repeating it despite
my protestations." Letter from George E. Reedy to
the author, May 13, 1980.

Senate staff; Bill D. Moyers, ordained Baptist clergyman and theology graduate of Edinburgh, former Peace Corps administrator, and a kind of trouble-shooter for LBJ; and George Christian, former press secretary for Governors John Connally and Price Daniel of Texas, who worked with President Johnson in his final months.

George Reedy's View of the President's Media Relations--George Reedy, who everyone concedes was and is a brilliant man, served Lyndon B. Johnson as his Press Secretary after the departure of Salinger until Reedy was obliged to resign for reasons of health. While Reedy was able according to such Kennedy staff persons as Arthur Schlesinger Jr. and Pierre Salinger,[2] the Washington correspondent corps felt that he did not have the full confidence of President Johnson and therefore felt his effectiveness was impaired, through no fault of Reedy's but rather because of the President's mode of operating.[3]

In a correspondence with Mr. Reedy, this author discovered that compared to Press Secretaries who viewed the Press Secretary as a spokesman or "mouthpiece" for the President, Mr. Reedy had what was perhaps an unorthodox view of the position. It was apparently Mr. Reedy's view that rather than acting merely as a public relations person for the President, the Press Secretary should give out all possible information about the President with the expectation that the President would be treated fairly by the correspondent corps. That may have been an unfounded expectation, but it was apparently his belief.

---

[2]Comment based on interview with Schlesinger at City University of New York, July 1978, and interview with Salinger at ABC Bureau, 22 Avenue d'Eylau, Paris, September 1979.

[3]Based on interviews with Bob Schieffer, December 1978; Marquis Childs, October 1978, and Robert Pierpoint, August 1979.

Mr. Reedy commented: "You are quite correct in assuming that LBJ and I had differences of opinion about the press office. Far from being "pushed around", my problem is that I would NOT be pushed around. I regarded the press staff as primarily a service institution and thought that razzle-dazzle public relations would actually be harmful to the Presidency. LBJ, on the other hand, thought that the purpose of the office was to get his name in the newspapers. He had grossly exaggerated views on what Michelson had done for Roosevelt, Hagerty for Eisenhower and Salinger for Kennedy. We reached a complete stalemate and it is true that information was withheld from me because he wanted to save it and redesign it for "public relations". I also developed some strong reservations about the war in Viet Nam and about some of his Great Society programs (which I believed were raising expectations that could not be fulfilled as long as the war was going on and therefore would breed cynicism). My private expression of views served to increase the gulf between us."

It is the informed speculation of this author that in serving President Johnson and the White House press corps, Mr. Reedy had a classic case of role conflict. He felt an obligation to the President to serve him, but he felt an obligation to the news media to inform them as fully as possible. This eventually put Mr. Reedy in a difficult situation, so difficult that even years later he indicated that the time of his resignation from the White House was perhaps the most difficult time of his life.

After leaving the White House, Mr. Reedy wrote from his deep fund of Washington experience and personal knowledge that there is a tendency of White House staff persons to insulate the President.[4]

---

[4]See George E. Reedy, Twilight of the Presidency (Cleveland: World Publishing Co., 1970).

The book published by Mr. Reedy indicated that every President is subject to this kind of insulation from reality, because he is surrounded by courtiers who identify their personal interest with his own. This is generally true in Washington, in the opinion of this author, who has found that some Senators have been surrounded by overprotective staffs who have been counterproductive to the interests of their bosses.[5]

Reedy's relationship with President Lyndon Johnson may have to unfold when historians have access to all relevant documents, but it is certain that Reedy was in Johnson's employ for many years, both in the Senate and in the White House. Most news people I interviewed indicated that Johnson had a tendency to "bully" Reedy, and they were most sympathetic with Reedy.

Marquis Childs tells of attending press briefings with Reedy during the Johnson era when President Johnson kept an open microphone in the White House briefing room while Reedy was briefing the media correspondents. Johnson maintained a loudspeaker in the Oval Office by which means he could keep track of Reedy's every action if he so desired.

---

[5]Mr. Reedy commented, ". . .you wonder why I do not believe that Senators are isolated by their staffs in the same manner as Presidents. This is because Senators have peers--99 other human beings who argue with them every day. Senatorial staffs would play the same role as White House staffs if they could. But they cannot do so when their principal must step out on the floor of the Senate every day and hear some harsh truths. There are times, of course, when officious staff members separate their Senator--to his detriment--from the public but such Senators do not last." Mr. Reedy's comments in letter to author, May 13, 1980.

According to Childs, the columnist:

"George Reedy suffered from a lack of confidence on the part of his principal (President Johnson). Johnson had a loudspeaker that piped Reedy's press conferences into Johnson's private office. He (Johnson) monitored them. On occasion he would rush out into Reedy's office to add his own comments. Poor Reedy just suffered hell."[6]

It is no wonder that years later Reedy still has a painful memory of his relationship with Johnson.

Mr. Reedy believes the story which Childs related is apocryphal. He explained: "(This story) rests upon one incident in which the President called me during a briefing and I was able to get an answer to a question that was not anticipated. The incident was not repeated even though in press mythology it was supposed to be a regular occurrence. I believe it was a coincidence because in conferences with the President after my press briefings he never betrayed any knowledge of what had happened. I believe I knew him well enough by that time that he could not deceive me on such a subject. I should add, however, that it would have been quite possible for the office to be bugged without my knowledge. The President can do many things of which his direct assistants are completely ignorant."[7]

Reedy's relationship with the White House media correspondents was undermined because of the problem mentioned by columnist Childs, but White House staff people and correspondents generally respected Reedy's ability. They merely felt that

---

[6]Interview with Marquis Childs, United Feature Syndicate and St. Louis Post-Dispatch columnist, at Post-Dispatch Washington Bureau, 1701 Pennsylvania, N.W., Washington, Friday, October 27, 1978.

[7]George E. Reedy in letter to author, May 13, 1980.

Johnson did not develop a close relationship with Reedy in the sense of giving him information the press could use. This perhaps grew out of President Johnson's native caution and penchant for secrecy. In spite of great efforts to get positive media coverage Johnson never fully succeeded, even in the full bloom of the Great Society. In an article previously published, this author noted that if LBJ ever had a "honeymoon" with the news media, it effectively ended after the 1964 election contest with Goldwater.[8] Johnson got some positive coverage during the period of the 89th Congress when Great Society legislation was being approved overwhelmingly, but even then the media were beginning to write negatively about Johnson's Vietnam policy. (The Gulf of Tonkin episode occurred in August 1964, and during the 1964 campaign LBJ promised "no wider war".)

Reedy has to be considered as an outstanding man whose talents were simply not effectively used by President Johnson. President Johnson had many positive qualities, but one of them was not to refrain always from abusing his staff.

Reedy's successor as Press Secretary, while controversial at times, was deemed rather successful by others such as Pierre Salinger who gave him high marks, as well as by Childs who felt Moyers was effective.[9]

Bill Moyers was a most capable Press Secretary, but he suffered from the problem which has beset other Press Secretaries, perhaps most recently Jody Powell--the fact that he was called on by the President to act as a trouble-shooter and versatile

---

[8]"The Myth of the Johnson Credibility Gap", scheduled for 1980 publication in _Presidential Studies Quarterly_.

[9]Childs interview, Washington, October 1978, and Salinger interview, Paris, September 1979.

aide in areas outside press relations. Moyers was gifted and eloquent, but at this phase of his career some felt he was capable of self-promotion. President Johnson was said to have complained at the time of Moyers' resignation that his (LBJ's) poll ratings were high when Moyers started working for him and that they had gone down during Moyers' tenure--surely a non sequitur.

Moyers' duties with the media sometimes did conflict with his other staff assignments; he was capable and had a varied background of experience. Thus he and staffers like Jack Valenti were relied on a great deal by President Johnson. Other staff members like Walt Whitman Rostow had a great deal of respect for Moyers' capabilities.[10]

Moyers' work in journalism since his White House days has included documentary work for the Columbia Broadcasting System and for the Public Broadcasting Service.

During his time with PBS, Moyers has interviewed a number of prominent figures, including David Rockefeller of the Chase Manhattan Bank in New York City.

On November 13, 1978, Moyers questioned President Jimmy Carter in a one-hour PBS interview, which covered both foreign and domestic policy questions, as well as relations between the White House and the news media.

From that interview transcript, furnished through the courtesy of the Democratic National Committee, I have selected some portions dealing with White House-media relations.

---

[10]Interview with Walt Whitman Rostow, in his office at the Lyndon Baines Johnson Library, Austin, Texas, September 1978.

President Carter told Moyers the problem was
that "at Camp David we didn't have daily press
briefings and this was the agreement when we
started here in Washington, that neither side
would make a direct statement to the press. As
you know, this has not been honored at all and it
has created enormous additional and unnecessary
problems for us."

Moyers asked, "You mean leaks from both gov-
ernments?"

The President replied, "Not just leaks, almost
every day I see interviews in the national television of at least one of the sides in the dispute. . .

Carter also told Moyers: "Quite often news
reports have been inaccurate when I think a simple
checking of the facts with a telephone call or a
personal inquiry could have prevented a serious
distortion of the news and also there is a sense
of doubt or even cynicism about the government and
about programs or proposals, brought about I am
sure by the Vietnam experience, of the fact that
the public was misled during Watergate and perhaps
even CIA, as I mentioned earlier.

"But I think that a lot of that was caused by
my relative inaccessability and by the lack of
knowledge on my part of the press and vice versa.
And in the last few months we have taken steps to
make sure that we understand each other better,
so that I have an ability and my Cabinet Members
have an ability to present the facts clearly to
the American people through the press and vice
versa."

Moyers asked, "Is this the work of your media
czar, Mr. Rafshoon? What did he tell you as to how
to get the message out?"

The President replied, "It was a common belief
that all of us had that we needed to have a clearer
access to the public through the press in an undis-
torted way, a truthful way, not to try to cover up

any mistakes we made and also to have it understood among those who report the news, that they
can have access to me or to Jody Powell, to Hamilton Jordan, to Members of the Cabinet or others
if there is a question that arises approaching a
deadline that they can make a telephone call and
say is this or is this not accurate.

"We all recognize the devastating consequences
of ever making a misleading statement or telling
a falsehood because our credibility would be
damaged and we have bent over backwards not to
do that."[11]

Moyers went to the White House after a brief
career in the Southern Baptist ministry and a period of study at Edinburgh, plus a time as a Peace
Corps official working with Sargent Shriver.
Moyers left the White House in late 1966 after
having succeeded Reedy about 18 months earlier.
His White House duties were far more comprehensive than only running the White House Press Office.
Moyers was a true generalist in the tradition of
White House aides. He went from the White House
to Newsday, a Long Island daily newspaper, to become its publisher. Since leaving Newsday, he
has been with the Public Broadcasting Service,
then with the Columbia Broadcasting System, and
once again with PBS. He is now with PBS and is
widely known for "Bill Moyers' Journal", a regular
feature on the public network. His journalistic
interests are wide-ranging. In the early 1970's
he wrote a book entitled Listening to America.[12]

In writing this book, Moyers took readings
of the political and social climate in such varied

[11]Bill Moyers' interview with President Carter, PBS Network, November 13, 1978.

[12]Bill Moyers, Listening to America: A
Traveler Rediscovers His Country (New York:
Harper's Magazine Press, 1971).

communities as Hartford, Connecticut; Richmond,
Indiana; Yellow Springs, Ohio; East Gary, Indiana;
Lawrence, Kansas; Denver; Cheyenne, Wyoming; Pine
Bluffs and Clear Creek, Wyoming; Bondurant, Wyoming;
Idaho Falls and Cascade, Idaho; Colfax and Seattle,
Washington; San Francisco; Los Angeles; Mathis,
Houston and Beaumont, Texas; Little Rock, Arkansas;
Johnsonville, South Carolina, and Washington, D.C.

Moyers summarized his findings on his journey
around the country (a Charles Kurault-like trip)
by stating:

"There is a myth that the decent thing has
almost always prevailed in America when the issues
were clearly put to the people. It may not always
happen. I found among people an impatience, an
intemperance, an isolation which invites opportun-
ists who promise too much and castigate too many.
And I came back with questions. Can the country
be wise if it hears no wisdom? Can it be tolerant
is it sees no tolerance? Can those people I met
escape their isolation if no one listens?"[13]

Eight years later, Moyers told an audience
in Toledo, Ohio, that he found the anger and
proneness to protest of the early 1970's had
turned into a mood of resignation, a recognition
that the American standard of living would decline,
a feeling of inability to affect the social and
political environment.[14]

Moyers has done some distinguished television
journalism while with CBS and PBS. One of his
CBS documentaries dealt with the Bay of Pigs and
the evolution of events in Cuba, another with
Vietnam policy. He has been given a largely free
hand in doing documentaries with PBS and has been
a recipient of awards for some of these.

_____

[13]Moyers, op. cit., p. 379.

[14]Comment based on Moyers' address to University of Toledo Friends of the Library, Inverness
Club, Toledo, September 1979.

David Halberstam says of Moyers' departure
from CBS that he was told by William S. Paley,
chief of CBS, that "the minute is too expensive
now" for Paley to allow Moyers to have a regular
documentary slot with CBS News, generally considered to be the most professional news network in
commercial television. Paley and CBS have denied
Halberstam's quotation. Moyers had no comment.[15]

Moyers has also participated in several symposia held for former Press Secretaries. A similar
one was held in Austin, Texas, under the sponsorship of the LBJ School of Public Affairs of
the University of Texas.   Another was held at
Gonzaga University, Gonzaga, Washington, and was
attended by Reedy and Salinger.

George Christian: Press Secretary as White
House Spokesman--George Christian lacked the flam-
boyance of Reedy or the intellectuality of Moyers,
but in a personal interview he projects a solidity
and integrity which are not always found in politics.

Here are some of Christian's views excerpted
from a 1978 personal interview:[16]

"(The Press Secretary)'s got a little bit
broader role today than existed at the time I was
there. This is the way it ought to be. This is
why a Press Secretary can do more to report for
reporters on things they're not privileged to be
involved in. He ought to be their eyes and ears
far more than he really is. But there is a time
bind. A lot of what goes on in the White House

---

[15]See David Halberstam, The Powers That Be
(New York: Random House, 1978).

[16]Interview with George Christian, former
Press Secretary to President Johnson, in Mr.
Christian's office, American Bank Tower, Austin,
Texas, Monday, August 28, 1978.

ought to be reported, would be helpful to the President and put him in a proper perspective for the people. Almost everything the White House correspondents get, they're spoon fed. There's no reason for not giving them more. I used to question why a lot of things we were doing were not made public. Accounts of Presidential decision-making eventually get out.

"There's a lot more that could be done on a daily basis to let the public know how the President reaches a decision. There's a lot of information that could be made available to them that isn't. A lot of it remains totally private, sort of falls between the cracks. There's very little danger of violating national security in most cases. Not enough attention is paid in the White House to making the decision-making process available to the press. There's too much fear you'll be misunderstood, and too much of an artificial atmosphere of decision-making. This situation has existed practically forever. The people don't look on a President as infallible--he's a man groping for answers to problems. When the public is not given a clear picture of the President and his problems, they have nothing on which to base confidence in him.

"The idea of an 'open government and an open White House' is a cliche. But despite these statements, the public usually knows just what the President wants them to know. It's better to reveal the facts in the normal course of events and let the public have a feel for what he (the President) is really doing. The public just sees the tip of the iceberg.

"The same wording and the same techniques have been used to let information helpful to the President trickle out. The press has become more cynical and has made the job of the Press Secretary more difficult from Ziegler to Powell. I believe the structure of the White House communications program is in a rut that followed Jim Hagerty's pattern.

50

"Certain things have been tried. Nixon tried
to get a better image by going to the press around
the country and (to) create better judgments
around the country on his administration (in effect, going over the heads of the Washington press
corps). Herb Klein was widely respected. Many
editors felt before he left, that he wasn't sitting
next to the throne and involved with the President
every day in what he was doing. The Powell-Raf-
shoon operation may or may not be good; it's too
early to tell. Ever since Johnson, there's been
a lot of experimentation. Manufacturing of events
in order to satisfy a public need for a President
they feel they can trust. So maybe this can be
unnecessary if a President can do his job well e-
nough.

"President Kennedy didn't have to create
this. He had a natural ability to deal with his
constituency. He had a keener political sense
than most presidents and knew how to sell himself. Everybody since then has tended to compare
himself to the Kennedy style and fret about not
being as adept at capturing the public's imagination. This has afflicted every President since
Kennedy. Nothing bugs a President more than to
feel he's not respected or believed. There's a
natural jealousy of JFK's ability in this particular arena. All worry about it too much and
create an artificial atmosphere that's not really
reflective of their own character or ability or
way of running the Presidency. When a President
has to 'ham it up' for public consumption, this
has always failed.

"Sometimes it may be a simple thing. President Johnson wanted to wear contact lenses in
his public appearances, but he had great difficulty handling this. It was not his way of handling
his duties. He had some of the finest oratory of
any President, but he didn't always communicate it
effectively. He gave guideposts for the country.
The image he wanted really hadn't stuck, he did
so much. The people were overwhelmed by LBJ. I've
seen little out of Nixon, Ford or Carter as yet.

51

"Going to China was Nixon's thing. They only
come across well when they do their own thing.
He knew it had to be done and he'd wanted to do
it even before he became President. The country
welcomed this from Nixon. We get flashes of when
a leader suddenly becomes a world statesman.
The primary cause of this country's decline in
recent years is a lack of this kind of leadership.
Our Presidents haven't displayed national leadership the rest of the world can look up to. The
high water mark of the U.S. in world affairs was
Kennedy in Berlin or the Cuban missile crisis.
Since then in fits and spurts we've been able to
be at the top of the heap as a nation again, but
we're not usually where we should be. Also in our
time there are no American heroes today. . . .

"I'm sure my experience with Governors Daniel
and Connally helped me at the White House. This
is partly why they accepted me. They knew I was
not totally ignorant of executive politics. This
was not always true of others, although it is
doubtless true that James Hagerty's experience
with Governor Dewey of New York helped him.
This work for Daniel and Connally was a lot different in some ways but from the standpoint of preparation there was an advantage of having been a
statehouse Press Secretary. You're just working
on a larger scale in Washington. My newspaper
background was helpful; a Press Secretary ought
to be able to see a reporter's point of view. . . .

(About Jody Powell) "We couldn't have had a
Press Secretary like him under Nixon, but Carter
and Powell are well suited to each other. They
have confidence in each other. Powell's had
trouble with press, of course, at times but he's
done a competent job for his boss.

"All Press Secretaries since Ziegler have
had a progressively tougher time. Press Secretaries generally reflect the people they work for.
Their style will be shaped by the Presidents
they work for, or they won't be there long.

"The last year of LBJ's tenure the Presidency changed direction; I knew Reedy and Moyers well, and perhaps I was more reticent than they were; Bill Moyers had verbal skills, I was more of a writer.

(About Jerald terHorst) "Jerry terHorst was too good a reporter to be able to handle the situation of the pardon and he did what he had to do to uphold his principles."

George Christian's reputation for competence as a press secretary was widespread. He was considered by the Washington correspondent corps to have had the confidence of President Johnson and to have given accurately the President's views of current issues. As noted by Pierre Salinger, Christian was guided by the wishes of the President and thus avoided controversies which have plagued some who have been Press Secretary.

Christian's tenure may have been less controversial than that of his predecessors, both Reedy and Moyers, because of the fact that when Christian took over the Press Secretary's duties many of the Vietnam controversies had begun to subside. He was serving during the Tet offensive of 1968 and at the time Walter Cronkite indicated the war was turning against the United States, but because he accurately reflected LBJ's thinking and exhibited loyalty to the President, he won the respect of both President Johnson and the press corps. Christian was considered a good craftsman and an able Press Secretary.

Special Problems of the Johnson Press Secretaries--The special problems of all the Johnson press secretaries, but especially of Reedy and Moyers, related to some extent to President Johnson's own "credibility gap", a personal matter that would have made any Press Secretary's role difficult.

Reedy's feeling that the press deserved the truth is commendable, but it came into conflict

with Johnson's view that in the national interest
partial truth is sometimes necessary in media relations. In the case of Moyers, a friction developed between him and Johnson as well. Again this
perhaps was more the fault of the President than his
Press Secretary; Lyndon Johnson was a gifted man
but he was also a difficult man to work for--
demanding and petulant one day, and compassionate
and forgiving the next day.

When one speaks of Johnson's "credibility
gap", it's necessary to ask: How unusual is this?
President Kennedy was accused by the opposition
of "news management"; President Eisenhower was
sometimes charged with using confusing syntax to
obfuscate; FDR was sometimes accused of using
repartee with reporters to obscure facts he didn't
want known. More recently, Carter and Nixon have
both been criticized for reducing the frequency
of news conferences when their popularity curve
in the surveys was declining. So every President
may have a credibility gap to some extent.

It is possible to conclude that Johnson's
media "honeymoon"--to the extent that he had one
at all--ended after the 1964 election. The phase
of sympathy for the burden he took on without
warning after the Kennedy assassination, and the
period of media fear of Senator Goldwater's
military policies (through the election) caused
the media in general to treat President Johnson
kindly. After the Vietnam escalation began
things were never the same again.

But similar points in other Administrations
can be noted--e.g., the Lance Case in the Carter
Administration; the Agnew attacks on the press and
television in the Nixon era; the Cuban missile
crisis in the Kennedy era when a Defense Department spokesman maintained that there are situations in which it is necessary "to lie for one's
country". So Johnson is not sui generis. It is
true that he, Nixon, Hoover and perhaps Wilson
after his 1919 illness (during the so-called
Regency of Edith Bolling Galt Wilson) all "took

their lumps" from the news media. But Johnson contributed to this problem as the others did. Even as capable a trio of Press Secretaries as Reedy, Moyers and Christian could not protect Johnson from himself. Despite this, Johnson had other skills--especially legislative leadership ones--so media relations should not be looked at in isolated fashion.

In a sense, it could probably be said that there was some improvement in media relations of the Johnson Administration after the President announced his impending retirement in 1968 and also announced his plans for peace negotiations with the North Vietnamese in Paris.

This is only relative however. The conduct of the Democratic National Convention in Chicago drew bad coverage for both the Johnson Administration and Hubert Humphrey, the nominee and incumbent Democratic Vice President. However, since LBJ was considered a "lame duck", the criticism of him lacked the bitterness which had previously been present. Also George Christian was a very astute and skillful Press Secretary and he may have smoothed the roiled waters somewhat.

In general then, Johnson after a short "honeymoon" and a smooth beginning had stormy media relations during most of the Reedy and Moyers tenure and even occasionally during Christian's tenure in the Press Office. As was the case with other Presidents, the President himself usually got the blame rather than his Press Secretaries. Johnson's Press Secretaries were all respected as professionals; Christian and Moyers were felt to have the confidence of the President, and it was really the President himself who put Reedy in an almost untenable position. Even years later, it was painful for Reedy to discuss the subject as the author's correspondence with him indicated. And Reedy is still admired as a knowledgeable journalist and currently is held in esteem as a journalism educator (Nieman Professor of Journalism at Marquette

University School of Journalism in Milwaukee).

President Johnson simply lacked the public
relations touch, but no one tried harder than he.
He was a master of legislative maneuver, but less
skillful than Kennedy and Eisenhower in media relations.

Photo by Okamoto
Courtesy, Lyndon B. Johnson Library

A veteran of 30 years Capitol Hill service, George E. Reedy of the Johnson staff stressed the importance of experience in the White House in making judgments about the Press Secretary's office and its various incumbents.

Photo by Okamoto
Courtesy, Lyndon B. Johnson Library

Bill Moyers, former publisher of <u>Newsday</u> and onetime CBS correspondent, shown here with President Johnson and another aide, became developer of "Bill Moyers' Journal" for the Public Broadcasting Service after Johnson White House service.

Photo by Okamoto
Courtesy, Lyndon B. Johnson Library

George Christian (standing) had experience working with two Governors before he became President Johnson's last Press Secretary.

CHAPTER FOUR

PRESS SECRETARIES AND THEIR VIEW OF THE OFFICE (III):

RICHARD NIXON'S PRESS OFFICE (1969-1974)

Richard Nixon's Press Secretaries and
Communications Directors--In Richard Nixon's
White House (1969-1974), the President appointed
Ron Ziegler, a former aide to Herb Klein, as
Press Secretary, and Nixon also created the post
of Communications Director. This post was held
by Herb Klein, and the Deputy Communications
Director was Ken Clawson, formerly of the Toledo
Blade and Washington Post, who succeeded Klein
when Nixon dismissed him in 1973. Ziegler stayed
with Nixon until the 1974 resignation, but in the
final months, Ziegler took over the Communications
Director's job and Nixon had an acting Press
Secretary, Gerald Warren, who had worked on the
Press Office Staff under Ziegler.

Ron Ziegler came from an advertising agency
background as did H. R. Haldeman. As a young man,
the Louisville native had been a guide for Disneyland riverboat cruises. He then went into the
advertising and public relations field. After
the end of Nixon's term, Ziegler worked for Nixon
for a time at San Clemente, assisting the former
President with his memoirs, but eventually left
him and is currently working for an engineering
firm in the Washington area.[1]

Ron Ziegler: Press Secretary Outside the
Inner Circle--Ron Ziegler, who worked with H. R.

---

[1]See Richard Nixon, RN: The Memoirs of
Richard Nixon (New York: Warner Books, 1979),
pp. 298, 440, Vol. I; pp. 121-126, Vol. II.

Haldeman in Nixon campaigns and had worked with
Herb Klein in Nixon campaign press operations in
1968, became Nixon's Press Secretary. In Washington parlance, the "inner circle" (perhaps
drawn from the traffic pattern of such landmarks
as DuPont Circle, Thomas Circle and the others)
consists of the President's closest advisers and
aides. Of this group, Ziegler was not a member
even though he was required to have frequent
contact with the President as Press Secretary.
This may have been an asset to Ziegler as he never
became deeply involved in the Watergate scandals.
This is apparent because of his well-publicized
remark that the Watergate denials he had issued in
response to Washington _Post_ stories had become
"inoperative" when irrefutable facts had been
uncovered by the Washington correspondent corps.

Ziegler is a classic example of the spokesman-
type Press Secretary who is not a member of his
President's inner circle. That inner circle in
the first Nixon term included John Mitchell,
Nixon's 1968 campaign manager; H. R. Haldeman,
White House chief of staff (as loyal to Nixon
until Watergate as Hamilton Jordan is to President Carter), and John Ehrlichman, Nixon's chief
domestic adviser whose role paralleled that of
Joe Califano in the Johnson Administration.
Other frequently mentioned advisers were William
Safire, a speechwriter; Dr. Henry Kissinger,
national security affairs adviser; Dr. Arthur
Burns, a chairman of Nixon's Council of Economic
Advisers, and for a time John Connally, Secretary
of the Treasury in the latter Nixon years. An
intimate of Nixon was "Bebe" Rebozo, a Miami area
savings and loan company official who had a home
on Key Biscayne, near Miami, and was a neighbor
of Nixon's there.

An ironic thing about Ziegler's performance
as President Nixon's Press Secretary is that despite
his unpopularity with much of the working press,
some of whose members Nixon despised, Ziegler was
considered very good at the housekeeping part of

the Press Secretary's job. He got the correspondents onto their planes on time, kept their hotel reservations from being fouled up, and in general ran a "tight ship" as far as logistical arrangements for overseas travel or domestic travel with President Nixon was concerned. Such correspondents as Robert Pierpoint of CBS and Frank Cormier of the Associated Press have mentioned, however, that Ziegler was not very informative, and that he usually reflected faithfully the current White House line. He would never go beyond what the President authorized him to say. Successful Press Secretaries like George Christian and--to an extent--Ron Nessen were inclined to follow this same policy, but they never had the same kind of stormy relations with the media that Ziegler did. The animus however did not originate with Ziegler, in the author's opinion, but rather with the President he served and his bitter enemies in the media. Ziegler simply got caught in the cross-fire and probably did well to survive as long as he did, given the embittered Nixon-media relations.[2]

Ron Ziegler was not involved in the Watergate scandal simply because he was not told things the President and the chief aides did not want him to know. This may have saved him from criminal involvement; as a technician, Ziegler was rated satisfactory by some correspondents, but they held little respect for him because they did not feel that he was close to his principal. That is something which Marquis Childs felt was crucial for a good Press Secretary.[3]

---

[2] Comments about Ziegler's efficiency from interviews with Robert Pierpoint, August 1979, and Frank Cormier, July 1979. See also William E. Porter, Assault on the Media: The Nixon Years (Ann Arbor: University of Michigan Press, 1977).

[3] See previous reference to interview with Marquis W. Childs, St. Louis Post-Dispatch Bureau, Washington, October 1978.

Unlike some other Press Secretaries, Ziegler never has written a book about his experiences, although he told an interviewer, Dom Bonafede, that someday he might do so after all the Watergate books were published.[4] Ziegler admitted to Bonafede and also stated in a Gonzaga University Press Secretaries symposium, that he felt in the afterlight of his post-Nixon career that he had been "used". But he did not wish to elaborate on this because he obviously felt a good deal of loyalty to the discredited Nixon.[5]

At an Austin symposium with George Christian, Ron Nessen, Jerald terHorst and Gerald Warren, as well as with such media luminaries as Dan Rather of CBS and Frank Cormier of the AP, Ziegler admitted there was a cover-up of Watergate for quite some months. He also added: " . . . (The) decisions that had been made as to how to deal with Watergate had culminated in absolute failure . . ."[6]

I believe that Ziegler faithfully and accurately conveyed Nixon's views when he was permitted to do so. But there were times when he had been instructed to be uncommunicative, and this led to a lowering of his esteem, such as it was, with the White House correspondents. The view is almost unanimous that if a Press Secretary is close to his President and

---

[4]Dom Bonafede, "A Conversation With Ron Ziegler", Washington Journalism Review, Spring 1978, pp. 46-49.

[5]The Presidential Press Secretaries' Forum, April 1, 1978, Campus of Gonzaga University.

[6]Hoyt Purvis, ed., The Presidency and the Press (Austin, Texas: Lyndon B. Johnson School of Public Affairs, University of Texas, 1976), p. 103. Ziegler said relatively little and said he did not want to debate the issue. However, in the Bonafede interview, he was somewhat more forthcoming.

knows most of what is going on, and is willing to share a reasonable amount of this information with the media, he is doing a good job. Unfairly or not for Press Secretaries, if one of them is not close to his President and is kept in the dark a great deal, he will have little respect from the White House correspondents. Ziegler was viewed by some as having misplaced loyalty, and some felt he lacked the news background to be effective in the job. That he was carrying out Nixon's instructions, there can be little doubt.

One episode which illustrates the problems that Ziegler had in working for President Nixon occurred in late 1973 in New Orleans, where the President was attending a meeting. Because of a mixup in instructions, Ziegler led a group of media people to where Nixon was going and Ziegler and the correspondents began following Nixon. This angered the President, already under heavy pressure from his own party and the media; he turned Ziegler bodily around and sent him to tell the press to get the hell out. Ziegler obeyed. Such episodes rankled; this whole episode was displayed on all three networks, and if the author's recall is correct was described in excruciating detail on CBS by Dan Rather, never one of President Nixon's favorites (and ironically enough, not too popular with his fellow Texan, President Johnson).

Ziegler's own view at the time he was serving appears to be that he was hired to do a particular job for President Nixon, and he was a good soldier carrying out orders. Ziegler did pride himself on administering the Press Office in an efficient and effective manner; most White House correspondents I have interviewed would corroborate this statement.

Herb Klein as Communications Director--A loyal retainer of Richard Nixon was Herb Klein, who was his press aide when Nixon was Vice President under Dwight D. Eisenhower. Klein continued with Nixon and served him in the 1960 and 1968 campaigns, as well as in the ill-fated campaign for Governor of California in 1962.

When Nixon was elected President in 1968, he took Klein with him to the White House the following year. Klein was appointed Communications Director. His responsibilities had less to do with the day-to-day operations of the White House Press Office, and more to do with long range efforts to advance the administration's interests through the media.

Concerning the degree to which the media have provided responsible White House coverage, Mr. Klein stated at a 1976 symposium:

" . . . Over the last maybe 15 or 20 years there have been a few occasions when it seemed to me that inadvertently or advertently, one way or the other, emotion really crept through the Press Room, and a couple of times on a campaign. I think that was true at one point in 1960; I think it was true in the latter part of the Nixon Administration which would be borne out by transcripts in the briefings. I think it would be true after the Ford pardon of Nixon and on some other occasions with Ron Nessen. Reporters obviously are human and they do have emotions. But I think that a weakness is when those emotions become dominant in how the questions are asked or how the reporting is done, despite very great efforts to be highly professional and to go after the news. And I think it is detrimental . . . "[7]

In response to a statement made by Ziegler at the Austin symposium, Klein had a further comment. What Ziegler said was: "I think this is a timely period to address the role of the press and the office of the Presidency, because I think now we are in a period of some relaxation, some respite

_____

[7]Purvis, op. cit., p. 77.

from these volatile issues that we have had to deal with over these past 10 to 15 years. I think it is important for us to examine where we have been and where we want to go and what has evolved from these past years.

"We have a new form of journalism. Many people feel the office of the Presidency has become too powerful. And, of course, we now have concluded a period where the country is examining some of its basic institutions . . . "[8]

In response, Klein stated: "I think this is, as Ron Ziegler has said, a very important time to consider the relationship of the press and the Presidency and the Press Secretary. In today's age, it is certainly necessary for a President to communicate, if he is to govern. We have seen what has happened when both President Johnson and later President Nixon lost the confidence of the American people and their ability to communicate, and in the process, they really lost the ability to govern in the latter part of the time they spent in office.

"We have also seen, I believe, a change in what takes place between the press and press secretaries, and what takes place between the press and the President. Franklin Roosevelt could get away with telling a reporter to go sit in the corner and put a dunce hat on. Can you imagine a President doing that today? There would be a major rash of stories about a President who was trying to exert his will, or to downgrade the correspondent himself.

"I would hope that we can find a way to not only look at the press conference of the President, but also the daily briefings of the Press Secretary,

---

[8]Purvis, op. cit., p. 18.

which I think have gone beyond the matter of adversary relationships. Too often there is too much rancor as a part of those meetings—rancor which leads to a waste of time, rancor which does not really serve the purpose of getting news that the American public deserves and needs . . . "[9]

In any event, the division of the function of Communications Director and Press Secretary begun in the Nixon Administration was in effect followed during the Carter Administration, when for a time Gerald Rafshoon held the former job while Jody Powell was holding the latter. Thus we see how, functionally, some precedents are followed despite changes of party in the White House.

The departure of Klein from the White House was followed by the service of Clawson and Ziegler. The latter served in the Communications Director's office after his credibility as Press Secretary had been badly battered when he was obliged to declare some of the previous Watergate denials "inoperative".

With the departure of Ziegler from the Press Secretary's job, Gerald Warren served briefly as acting Press Secretary. Warren might be considered as a transitional Press Secretary.

Gerald Warren served as a moderator at the Austin symposium but did not make extensive remarks there on his service in the White House.

---

[9]Purvis, op. cit., p. 19. For another Nixon staff aide's view of the relationship between Klein and the President, see William Safire, Before the Fall: An Inside View of the Pre-Watergate White House (New York: Belmont Towers Books, 1975), pp. 343-361.

As for the relationship between the men who served Richard Nixon, one expert commented in 1975:

"It would appear that technological evolution and growth of potential and real Presidential power have caused a steady progression toward specialization in Presidential press relations, calling for image caretakers ever more specialized in the arts of mass persuasion, i.e., public relations, opinion formation, advertising, electronic media. Based on trends in the Nixon White House, one might affirm the movement toward specialization. Mr. Ziegler, a former advertising executive with no experience in professional news media, appears to gain power at the expense of Herbert Klein and other White House public (relations) staff members whose backgrounds are in professional journalism . . . "[10]

If one looks back to Stephen Early in the Roosevelt Administration and Hagerty in the Eisenhower Administration, it would be fair to say that Press Secretaries today do not automatically come from a journalistic background, although that may still occur. In the Carter White House, for example, Jody Powell--the object of a later chapter--has essentially a background in political science and extensive service on Governor Carter's staff.

To summarize, we find in the Nixon era an acrimonious relationship between the President and the press which probably went back many years.[11] One also finds the beginning of a distinction between the daily operational function of the Press

---

[10]Donald R. Burkholder, "The Caretakers of the Presidential Image," Presidential Studies Quarterly, V: 1, Winter 1975, p. 41.

[11]See the discussion of this in David Halberstam, The Powers That Be (New York: Random House, 1979).

Secretary and the more long-term function of a
Communications Director. Thus the nation has a
dual legacy from the Nixon era. Jimmy Carter and
his successors may continue to labor under the
difficulties bred by the former; the latter, as
suggested by Burkholder, may be attributable to
advances in communications technology.

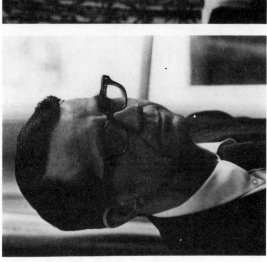

Courtesy, Nixon Project
The National Archives

Ronald L. Ziegler, right, with a background in advertising, was the Press
Secretary for President Richard Nixon and later became Communications
Director, when Gerald Warren, left, became Nixon's acting Press Secretary.

CHAPTER FIVE

PRESS SECRETARIES AND THEIR VIEW OF THE OFFICE (IV):

GERALD FORD'S PRESS OFFICE (1974-1977)

Jerald terHorst: Philosophy About Press Secretary as a White House Staff Adviser--During the period between August 9, 1974, and January 20, 1977, President Gerald R. Ford had two Press Secretaries. The first, who had a brief tenure prior to the pardon of Richard Nixon, was Jerald F. terHorst, for many years a Washington correspondent for the Detroit News. After serving Ford briefly, terHorst returned to that position which he still held at this writing.

The early operation of the White House Press Office under terHorst brought an almost euphoric treatment of President Ford by the media. Stories were told of how he went to the front door of his Alexandria home to pick up the morning newspaper, wearing a bathrobe and slippers, or of how shortly after his accession to the White House, he told the domestic staff he preferred to toast his own English muffins. These quite positive newspaper profiles about Ford's personality must have reflected the reality of the relief of nearly everyone in the correspondent corps about the departure of Richard Nixon after all those stormy years when both Nixon and the media felt persecuted, each by the other.

All this positive treatment of the President ended abruptly in a controversial episode which prompted terHorst's resignation. This occurred exactly a month after Ford began his term. The President returned home from a Sunday morning church service and in a spirit of forgiveness issued a proclamation of pardon for Richard Nixon. The Press Office had been given no advance notice; indeed it was a closely held secret until the final decision was made.

This prompted an outcry from those who felt the pardon amounted to a "double standard" of justice. Nixon was pardoned at a time when an indictment had been likely according to Judge John Sirica.[1]

Special prosecutor Leon Jaworsky, Archibald Cox's successor, also expressed similar views. Some analyses of the 1976 election indicated the pardon may have played a part in Ford's defeat.

The pardon is of interest in this analysis of Press Secretaries' part in the White House operation, because it exhibits how two quite different views of the Press Secretaries' role were held by terHorst and his successor, Ron Nessen.

Despite efforts to dissuade him by other members of the Ford staff, terHorst submitted his letter of resignation to the President.

The resignation letter, dated September 8, 1974, stated in part, ". . . (I)t is with great regret, after long soul-searching, that I must inform you that I cannot in good conscience support your decision to pardon former President Nixon even before he has been charged with the commission of a crime. As your spokesman, I do not know how I could credibly defend that action in the absence of a like decision to grant absolute pardon to the young men who evaded Vietnam military service as a matter of conscience and the absence of pardons

---

[1]Judge John J. Sirica, To Set the Record Straight: The Break-in, the Tapes, the Conspirators, the Pardon (New York: W.W. Norton & Co., 1979), pp. 231-239. Sirica suggests he at first felt the pardon may have been justified, but that he came to feel that Nixon "left office with the process for his removal incomplete" and admitted to the "lingering feeling that . . . Nixon did manage to keep himself above the law . . ." (pp. 234, 235).

for former aides and associates of Mr. Nixon who have been charged with crimes--and imprisoned-- stemming from the same Watergate situation. These are also men whose reputations and families have been grievously injured. Try as I can, it is impossible to conclude that the former President is more deserving of mercy than persons of lesser station in life whose offenses have had far less effect on our national well-being . . . ."[2]

The terHorst resignation letter reflects the former Press Secretary's view that no presidential spokesman can serve in good conscience without some input into such decisions as that of the pardon, and also that no spokesman can give loyalty to a President with whose major policy positions he differs. This view is not shared by everyone who has served as Press Secretary. As previous interview material indicated, some Press Secretaries have taken the view of Pierre Salinger that as long as they have input into the presidential decision they could accept it once made and give their loyalty under those circumstances.[3]

The third view, which will be discussed in more detail when Ron Nessen's tenure is considered, is that the Press Secretary is a spokesman for the President, whatever decisions are made by the President. Therefore loyalty to the President must be the guiding principle.

It appears that conflicting loyalties to the press corps and to President Ford were involved in terHorst's case, and that the former won out because of terHorst's long-standing attitude as a professional journalist. Before leaving the sub-

---

[2]Jerald terHorst, _Gerald Ford and the Future of the Presidency_ (New York: The Third Press, 1974), p. 236.

[3]Personal interview with Pierre Salinger, cited in Chapter Two, conducted at ABC News Bureau, Paris, September 18, 1979.

ject, it's necessary to consider President Ford's view since the resignation prompted great disappointment and sadness on his part in a situation in which the President clearly felt he had done the right thing.

Ford of course looked at the matter from a different vantage point. The Nixon matter was absorbing too much of his time, and was interfering with his management of the nation's affairs, he felt.

After detailing in his memoirs the consideration of the issue which preceded the pardon, Ford related his conversation with terHorst on learning of the latter's resignation. The President told terHorst, according to Ford's account, "Jerry, I regret this. I think you've made a mistake. But I respect your views, and I'm sorry if there was any misunderstanding. As to the pardon, it was a decision I felt I had to make. I've made it and I'm going to stick with it. I hope that you will reconsider and change your mind."

TerHorst replied that his decision was final and noted his views in the letter to the President from which I've quoted above.[4]

The whole matter is put in a somewhat different light in the column published by John Osborne, New Republic White House correspondent and a long-time White House observer. Perhaps it can best be summarized in these two brief excerpts:

". . . I'm glad that President Ford pardoned former President Nixon. I hoped that Mr. Ford would do it before he did it and I'm sorry only that he did it in the worst possible way. . . ."

After detailing pre-pardon consultations

---

[4]See also Gerald R. Ford, A Time to Heal: The Autobiography of Gerald R. Ford (New York: Harper & Row/Reader's Digest Association, 1979), p. 176.

between Ford and his closest aides, Osborne commented: "Mr. Ford's Press Secretary and friend of 25 years, Jerry terHorst, resigned in protest. A matter of principle, he said. He is suspected at the White House of wanting out anyhow and of using the pardon as a pretext. Mr. Ford believed it was indeed an act of principle. 'You just don't understand these evangelical Michigan Dutchmen', he told an outraged loyalist."[5]

Ron Nessen: Acceptance of Spokesman Role for Press Secretary--Turning to the television White House contingent, President Ford selected as terHorst's successor an NBC correspondent, Ron Nessen, whom he had known and come to like while he was Vice President.

It's been mentioned previously that Nessen conceived of the Press Secretary's job as essentially that of a technician whose task is to get news to the public about his boss's decisions. But a few brief excerpts from Nessen's account of his White House service might better sum up his feelings.

After describing the circumstances of the Nixon pardon, Nessen commented:

"Whatever my personal feelings about it, the President's announcement of the pardon changed my life, because it caused Jerry terHorst to resign as Press Secretary. . . .

"Some Ford staff members thought terHorst resigned because Philip Buchen, the President's legal counsel, had misled him a few days earlier by denying that a pardon was in the works. That caused the popular and conscientious terHorst innocently to mislead a reporter who'd gotten a

---

[5]John Osborne, "The Pardon", New Republic column, September 28, 1974, reprinted in John Osborne, White House Watch: The Ford Years (Washington: New Republic Books, 1977), pp. 1-7.

tip that a pardon was imminent. Other Ford aides thought terHorst was simply overwhelmed by the amount of work and pressure in the Press Office and took the first convenient occasion to bail out. But whatever terHorst's reasons, his timing bothered Ford enormously. Ford never forgave terHorst for quitting at such a crucial moment, referring to his former friend in private conversations afterward as 'that son of a bitch'.

"Nevertheless, terHorst's successor would have a tough act to follow. In fact, two tough acts to follow. The new man would have to live down Ziegler and live up to terHorst. . . ."[6]

Nessen's tenure as Press Secretary with Ford between September 1974 and January 1977 extended over a period when the White House was beset with many difficult issues and problems.

This period saw the Vladivostok summit between President Ford and Secretary Brezhnev, as well as the Helsinki European Security Conference of 1975 and the Angola crisis. It was also a time when Secretary of State Henry Kissinger exhibited much nervousness about "Eurocommunism" following the Portugese revolution. In domestic terms the impact of the energy crisis, the New York City fiscal crisis, the recession of 1975 and many other matters vied for the President's attention.

Other episodes described by Nessen included the Mayaguez episode of the seizure of an American ship and its recapture in 1975, the Cabinet shakeup in fall 1975 (largely forgotten by many in the Washington press corps at the time of the Carter 1979 Cabinet shakeup), the Bicentennial observance and of course the 1976 election which absorbed much of Ford's attention because of the challenge of former California Governor Ronald Reagan and the close contest with former Governor Jimmy Carter

---

[6]Ron Nessen, It Sure Looks Different from the Inside (Chicago: Playboy Press, 1978), p. 10.

of Georgia.

Some of Nessen's views about the Ford Administration can be gained from these excerpts from an interview which was included at the end of Nessen's book:

" . . . He (President Ford) presided over the end of the Vietnam war in a way that began to heal the divisions the war had caused in American society. And he insisted, against initial congres - sional and public opposition on fulfilling a humanitarian obligation to the refugees. With the <u>Mayaguez</u> rescue he demonstrated to potential adversaries that the United States would stand up for its rights in Asia despite the ill-fated Indochina adventure . . . Ford cut the inflation rate by more than half. He guided the nation out of the deepest recession since the Thirties with policies that stimulated the economy to recover in a sound, steady way . . . Ford supervised the public disclosures of excesses by the CIA, FBI and other intelligence and investigative agencies. Then, he proposed reforms to prevent future abuses without wrecking essential government functions. Ford also recruited people of extraordinarily high caliber for top posts in government. . . ."[7]

When asked for the names of some of the stronger appointees named by President Ford, Nessen suggested Associate Justice John Paul Stevens, the late Vice President Nelson Rockefeller, Attorney General Edward Levi, HUD Secretary Carla Hills and Transportation Secretary William Coleman.[8]

Besides his comments while serving and in his book, Nessen has participated in occasional symposiums in which Press Secretaries for various Presidents have taken part. During these appearances, he has expressed his viewpoint on other public issues. For instance, in the Austin sym-

---

[7]Nessen, <u>op. cit.</u>, pp. 356, 357.

[8]Nessen, <u>op. cit.</u>, p. 357.

posium, Nessen disputed the belief by some that the Washington correspondent corps has superior ability to that of the grass roots media. Answering a question from Hugh Sidey, Nessen commented:

"First, when I took this job, I asked the President how much time each week he wanted to spend on news conferences, and so forth. And he said, 'Well, let's try and hour and a half a week', which is really more than 15 minutes a day. And as it has turned out, it has been more than an hour and a half a week.

"I do not agree . . . that there are some special qualities that the reporters who are based each day at the White House have which other reporters do not have. In fact, quite the opposite. I think the recent interviews the President has given to reporters, for instance, from Texas newspapers and Texas television stations and news conferences out and around the country in different cities--I think those reporters, by their questions, tough questions, have indicated that they have a pretty good grasp of what their readers and viewers are interested in and perhaps an even better grasp than the people who have been based for 20 and 25 years in the isolation of the White House. We have talked about the isolated President, maybe we should also talk about the isolated White House correspondent.

"But, seriously, I think that the reporters out and around the country ask good questions and do represent the interests and curiosities of their readers and their viewers."[9]

At the same symposium, Dan Rather of CBS replied to Nessen and other participants by stating:

---

[9]Hoyt Purvis, ed., The Presidency and the Press (Austin, Texas: Lyndon B. Johnson School of Public Affairs, University of Texas at Austin, 1976), p. 25.

"I can think of no more worthy subject to deal
with than this idea, that I think increasingly under recent Presidents the White House Press Office
and the briefing room itself have become propaganda pulpits. This has got to stop one way or
the other. If any of us, given all of our prejudices and these prisms I spoke of, are to get
anywhere near the truth, this has simply got to
stop.

"Now, how this came to be, why it is, is something that increasingly interests me. I do not
have all the answers to it. But I do think that
it has become, over the last decade, a propaganda
pulpit in which the Press Secretary has ceased to
even envision himself as an honest broker of information. If, as some of you . . . ask, 'What is
it you want out of a Press Secretary?' My answer
as a reporter is, 'I would hope that within the
bounds of your human limitations that you would
try to be an honest broker of information.'. . .

"Ron Nessen talked about the adversary relationship. Ron, I think you had better get back on
our side of the table quickly because I think you
strayed a bit from what you and I both know to be
the truth--that reporters and Presidents are not
made to get along with one another. Part of our
job as reporters, not our only job, but part of
our job is to be watchdogs, not attack dogs, on
the one hand, and certainly not lap dogs on the
other, but watchdogs. . . ."[10]

Ford's Incumbency and the Slow Improvement of
Media Relations--Despite the bitterness of the
Nixon era which carried over to some extent into
the Ford period after the pardon, there was perhaps a gradual improvement in media relations
before Gerald Ford left the White House. Perhaps
the challenge to him in the 1976 primaries and
his role as national host during the Bicentennial

---

[10]Purvis, op. cit., pp. 27-29.

may have brought about some changes. Perhaps it was all part of the healing process which gave the title to Ford's memoirs and which caused President Jimmy Carter to acknowledge Ford's role in "healing our land" in his 1977 inaugural. At any rate, while some tensions continued to exist, especially after the Nixon pardon, there did appear to be some improvement in White House relations with the media in the two and a half years of the Ford Presidency.

President Ford used several formats for his news conferences. He seemed to prefer to use the East Room of the White House; there was precedent for this as Lyndon Johnson had done so.

Ford also extended a trend which had begun under his immediate predecessor. Referred to in the Austin symposium, this trend was that of going out to the country and having contact with the grass roots reporters and photographers in communities outside Washington. To some extent it has been followed with President Carter's town meeting format. The basic problem suggested by senior correspondent Frank Cormier remains, however. That is the problem that the White House Press Office as currently staffed is not fully enough manned to permit extensive use of this technique.[11]

Various efforts were made at restoring White House credibility during the Ford era. An effort was made to make the White House somewhat more open, in general. Following the example of President Truman a generation earlier, for instance, President Ford permitted author John Hersey to visit the White House for the writing of a book about a typical day in the President's schedule.[12]

---

[11]Interview with Frank Cormier, Associated Press senior White House correspondent, Washington, July 19, 1979.

[12]See John Hersey, The President (New York: Alfred A. Knopf, 1975).

This also followed an earlier example in that the Kennedy Administration had admitted television correspondents to complete an ABC special about civil rights decision-making in the tense summer months of 1963.

President Ford did participate with correspondents in small group interviews, as had each of his predecessors since Kennedy.

Some observers noted that despite all these efforts the thin-skinned response of Ron Nessen to correspondents hampered the President's credibility effort. But there can be little doubt that despite frictions, there was noticeable improvement over the situation during the Nixon period.

Ford also suffered from a rather unfair stereotype perhaps best expressed in the comment once made facetiously by Lyndon Johnson when Ford was minority leader in the House, to the effect that he "couldn't chew gum and walk a straight line at the same time." Ford was not such a "klutz" but he was made to appear so. This was not helped by the fact that he was depicted by the news media as falling in the snow at Vail, his favorite skiing spot, or tumbling down an airliner ramp on his arrival at Vienna when an old "football knee" began acting up. This physical clumsiness symbolism somehow portrayed that here was a man who was clumsy about handling the nation's affairs and international diplomacy. Unfair as it may have been, it kept Ford from having the kind of rapport with the public he might have been expected to have.

The White House media did accompany Ford on his overseas travels. There was much comment along the lines described above when he appeared in a rented formal suit with the Emperor of Japan and the pants appeared several inches too short.

Despite all this, there was a considerable amount of sympathetic treatment at least of the goals

Ford was pursuing in overseas summits, the Helsinki conference, and visits to other foreign leaders.

The overseas coverage aspects of the White House correspondent corps' duties have been dis- cussed by Robert Pierpoint, who was asked to describe his participation in overseas coverage of the President in such places as Tokyo and Vienna. Pierpoint noted:

"It's not that much different. You're still covering the President but your job is basically the same. The focus is on foreign affairs, it's true, but we're generalists anyway. Sometimes problems exist. It may be more difficult to have access to information and to get information out to the public. There are some differences. Be- cause of time-zone differences you may work an 18- hour day overseas. In other ways, it's not much different than traveling domestically. The White House still charters a plane and the network pays. It takes more manpower."

Pierpoint, a former foreign correspondent, was asked whether he enjoyed traveling to cover the President or Vice President. His response: "I don't enjoy the travel that much because of the tremendous workload and time that's involved. We usually try to cover in infinite detail when the President is traveling overseas, moreso than when he's at home. I tend to consider it a chore, a burden. When I was a foreign correspondent, I loved to travel. There are some exceptions to this, of course. If you can go ahead of the President's party, as I recently did in Tokyo, and have more time to do the coverage, that's different. But you're working long hours every day under normal circumstances."[13]

It can be said in summary that President Ford

---

[13]Interview conducted by telephone with Robert Pierpoint, CBS News White House correspondent, August 6, 1979.

did some things to take the bitterness out of the
relationship between the White House and the media
It should also be added that the institutional
relationship between the two is likely to continue
to pit the two against each other in many instan-
ces--Presidents seeking to control the timing of
the release of information, while the media of all
kinds seek as much information as they can get.
One must also remember that the very nature of the
high-pressure news operation makes it inevitable
that some of the most controversial news will come
from elsewhere in Washington than the White House
itself. That was what happened with Woodward and
Bernstein.

Courtesy, Gerald R. Ford Library Project
The National Archives

Jerald F. terHorst of the Detroit News interrupted his service with the News
briefly to serve President Gerald R. Ford as Press Secretary.

Ronald Nessen left NBC to become President Ford's
Press Secretary after the Nixon pardon controversy.

CHAPTER SIX

PRESS SECRETARIES AND THEIR VIEW OF THE OFFICE (V):

JIMMY CARTER'S PRESS OFFICE (1977-PRESENT)

In analyzing the operation of the White House Press Office during the period since 1977, some evidence is already available. It tends to indicate that there is a kind of cyclical treatment of the President in the media, which perhaps sometimes resembles a roller-coaster. The Carter Administration got off to a relatively good start in media relations. This lasted for about six to eight months, when the Bert Lance controversy-- ending in Lance's resignation--embittered and exacerbated these relations somewhat.

The media relations of the Carter White House improved somewhat in 1978, although there was some feeling that coverage of overseas travels and the Camp David summit of that year was at times unduly restrictive.[1]

After that the up-and-down pattern continued, with a period in 1979 when White House personnel must have felt that the President was getting "ugly duckling" treatment while Senator Ted Kennedy was getting "kid glove" treatment from the media. This period probably ended with the active candidacy of Kennedy, and the turning point may have been when President Carter received relatively positive coverage of his participation in the dedication ceremonies for the John F. Kennedy Library at Columbia Point in Boston in October 1979.

---

[1]See references to Schieffer and Pierpoint interviews in Chapter Fourteen. See also William C. Spragens, "Television Network Coverage of the 1978 Camp David Summit", in William Adams, ed., Television News and the Middle East (forthcoming).

Jody Powell: Effectiveness With White House
Press Corps--While the relationship after the
Lance episode may never have been as positive as
before, White House correspondents since 1977 have
normally given Jody Powell, the Carter Press Secretary, credit for one attribute which is sine
qua non for effectiveness in the Press Secretary's
job. This is the ability of the Press Secretary
to be sufficiently close to the President that the
media find his statements reliable in that they
reflect the President's current thinking.

This has been the case with Jody Powell, who
with Hamilton Jordan has been close to President
Carter since Carter's gubernatorial term in
Georgia if not before.[2] It was also pointed out
that one of the difficulties that arises when the
President relies greatly on his Press Secretary
for other duties is that there may at times be an
accessibility problem.[3]

An exception to the mostly favorable reaction
to Powell's work in the Press Office probably is
found in a September 1977 comment by Newsweek
correspondent David M. Alpern, Lucy Howard,
Eleanor Clift and Thomas M. DeFrank of the Washington Bureau who stated of Powell:

"He came to the White House like a Southern
breeze, a press secretary who could make fun of
reporters, himself--even the President on occasion--
and still get the job done. After eight years of

---

[2] While it will be reflected in greater detail
in a later chapter, Pierpoint's view of Powell as
"one of the best press secretaries I've worked
with in terms of being a voice for the President"
is relevant here. See Chapter Fourteen.

[3] See in particular the reference by Frank
Cormier in Chapter Fourteen to the accessibility
problem in regard to Powell. Cormier found that
Powell "can be very good really, when you can get
to him." Interview with Cormier conducted July
15, 1979.

bitterness and distrust in the Ziegler-Nessen press operations, many correspondents believed Jody Powell to be the most promising Presidential spokesman in years. But in recent months, Bert Lance's tangled affairs have given Powell his first real test under fire, and the press secretary has lost some of his professional cool and credibility. At one recent press briefing, John Osborne of the New Republic told him publicly what many White House reporters had begun saying in private. 'You and your people', warned the courtly veteran correspondent, 'are just about ready to go over the wall on the Lance thing.'

"The Lance case has forced Powell and the press to face some facts of life. As Powell's good-old-boy banter gave way to nasty cracks, angry phone calls and sharp confrontations, members of the media were reminded again that the press secretary works for the President and not for them. . . ."[4]

The author has had opportunity to see Powell at work in various settings, not always in the same place. Pending receipt of comments by Powell on his initial four years with Carter in Washington, these observations can be made.

Powell was one of those attending a Washington Hilton fund-raising event for the President, a kind of $1,000 a plate birthday party for the President attended by many senators and congresspersons and definitely not a formal accasion insofar as working was concerned. On this occasion, both Powell and Hamilton Jordan were seen to be mixing among the crowd and both exhibited a great deal of affability to be expected on a social occasion.

---

[4]See "Jody Faces Life", in Newsweek, September 19, 1977, pp. 119, 120, quoted in William C. Spragens, The Presidency and the Mass Media in the Age of Television (Washington: University Press of America, 1978), p. 294.

A second occasion at which I saw Powell at work was at the Democratic Mid-term conference in Memphis in December 1978. He was touring the press facilities, simply on hand to be sure that no one needed any further assistance that he/she was not already getting.

The third occasion was a planned visit at the White House, originally intended for an interview. This was of necessity rescheduled. On this occasion, the author was informed by Powell about the resignation offers of the senior staff and entire Cabinet and the Press Office staff indicated that various correspondents would probably be available for conversations after they had completed the filing of their stories.

Jody Powell's role as Press Secretary was examined by David Brinkley of NBC in a December 1979 documentary. Brinkley commented: "Even up to Hoover's time, when he had a press conference, he would only accept written questions in advance, because he said, 'The President of the United States will not be questioned like a chicken thief by men whose names he does not even know.' More recently, Presidents have talked a great deal and not always truthfully. Two have left office believing the press had destroyed them."

Concerning the influence of the news media, Powell commented for NBC: "It is an awesome power in this country. In fact, there are probably few institutions in our nation that exercise as much power on a day to day continuing basis as does the press that covers the White House. And, of course, network television, because of the literally tens of millions of people that you reach every night has a power for good or for ill that probably has never been equalled at any other time in history."

Brinkley's documentary included comments from other correspondents: Judy Woodruff--"As a reporter I never feel that we are being told enough about what the President is doing. We have complained and complained and complained to Jody

Powell and anybody else who would listen, but as long as they feel that it's not in their interest to be accessible, as we would like them to be, they won't do that." Sam Donaldson--"I have no access to the policy makers here, except on their terms. Even though I have a badge it admits me only to Jody Powell's office. I can't go see Hamilton Jordan, stick my head in Stuart Eizenstadt's office, drop by Frank Moore's place and say 'What's going on today?'"

The documentary portrayed Powell in a meeting with reporters in his office, stating, "I certainly am not going to give an interview with the President on a particular subject to a reporter that I know doesn't have any idea on God's earth about what's involved in the subject. So I think that's legitimate. You don't cast your pearls before the swine, so to speak. But I don't consider that managing the news. I just consider that common sense."

Brinkley suggested that it was difficult to find a particular type of President that television helped more than any others.[5]

---

[5]Excerpts from transcript of David Brinkley documentary aired on NBC, December 26, 1979, pp. 61-63, 66, 67. For other views on Powell and his predecessors, see a section entitled "The Press and the Presidency", with contributions by Michael Grossman and Martha Kumar, Dom Bonafede, Jody Powell, Edmund Morris, and Carroll Kilpatrick (former Washington Post White House correspondent), in Washington Journalism Review. A cyclical analysis by Grossman and Kumar suggests that institutions involved cause three phases to occur in White House media relations--Alliance, Competition and Detachment. The latter does not seem to explain prolonged criticism of the Carter Administration. Washington Journalism Review, May 1980 (2: 3), pp. 41-56.

From general reports and impressions of
Powell's attitude toward the job of Press Secretary,
it appears that Powell is a bit more relaxed than
his immediate predecessors. He also is generally
viewed as a loyal spokesman for the President.
In one interview, a correspondent went so far in
praising the performance of Powell as to note
that in the Bert Lance affair, one of the most
controversial events in the first two years of the
Carter term, that while it was badly handled this
was largely the fault of the President and not of
his Press Secretary.[6]

Role of Jagoda and Rafshoon in Powell's Press
Office--The tenure of Barry Jagoda in the White
House Press Office covered approximately two years
prior to his departure in early 1979. Jagoda's
departure preceded the appointment of Gerald Rafshoon to head the communications function in the
White House and Rafshoon served there until his
return to Atlanta to participate in the communications aspects of the Carter-Mondale 1980 campaign.

As noted by Pierre Salinger, the broadcasting
function of the White House Press Office has become so important that a special section of the
Press Office now deals solely with television.[7]

Barry Jagoda, who worked in the 1976 Carter
campaign and who had broadcasting experience
with both NBC and CBS before his White House tour
of duty, noted that the Carter White House carried

------

[6]Interview with Robert Pierpoint, August 9,
1979. The CBS correspondent stated that the acrimonious exchanges were more the fault of the
President than of his Press Secretary. In the
Cormier interview, cited above, it appeared that
there was concern in the White House press corps
that the Carter Administration might be sliding
into the Ford-Nixon habit of emphasizing non-
Washington news coverage.

[7]Interview with Pierre Salinger, ABC News Bureau, 22 Avenue d'Eylau, Paris, September 18, 1979.

out the briefing function (internally for the President) in a more informal manner than other recent administrations.

One of the more interesting revelations during a 1977 interview with Jagoda, completed for an earlier book by this author, was the comment that the television adviser's role has evolved into a more policy-oriented kind of position. The television adviser's comment: "I find myself more involved in policy-making for communications. There has been a change here. This is something new. TV advisers in the past tended to worry about lens angles, makeup, etc. But my feeling is you can't outwit television; TV presents actuality and I think the President must project himself just as he is. Carter is very good at this, just being natural. He instinctively does the things he should do, such as to look at the camera if he is not looking at a questioner (the former in a less question-and-answer kind of format). I handle liaison with the networks and to some extent I am involved in questions of policy-making."

Jagoda also commented: "The most effective means of using TV is to have a grasp of questions which are in the public's mind (such as the energy issue). The best way he could use TV is if there were a crisis so the President can easily get a feeling of the public pulse."[8]

The beginning of Rafshoon's tenure as communications adviser for the President came at a time when new problems were arising. One of the more difficult of these was striking a balance between overexposure and underexposure. Rafshoon was hired because of his successful development of the television campaign for President Carter in 1976, and

---

[8]Interview with Barry Jagoda, television adviser and special assistant to President Carter, Old Executive Office Building, Washington, September 1, 1977, excerpted from material in William C. Spragens, op. cit., pp. 284-287.

the anticipation that he would eventually be working in a re-election campaign for the President. There are differences, however, in dealing with an incumbent President between elections and with a candidate.

Rafshoon was felt to be a good technician, but the problems which President Carter seemed to be having during this period lay in a public perception of some lack of effectiveness with the Congress in securing the adoption of important legislation. This may have been an incorrect perception, since 1979 statistics indicated that at least in terms of percentages of bills adopted in Congress, the Carter record was better than the overall record of the last Democratic incumbent, Lyndon Johnson, who had the reputation of being a legislative wizard.[9]

Rafshoon's working relationship with Powell and with President Carter was apparently a good one, since his departure was prompted not by any particular lack of confidence in his work, but because his expertise was deemed needed in the 1980 campaign.

In summary, it could be said that Powell appears to be among the four or five most effective Press Secretaries since the time of George Akerson, considered the first officially designated Press Secretary, who served during the Herbert Hoover Administration and who because of circumstances of the Great Depression, never really became as effective as most of his successors.[10]

---

[9]To some extent this may indicate the validity of the views of Richard Neustadt, who emphasized the importance of the Washington community and its perceptions of the President's ability. See Neustadt, Presidential Power, Third Revised Edition (New York: John Wiley & Sons, 1980).

[10]See Michael Medved, The Shadow Presidents: The Secret History of the Chief Executives and Their Top Aides (New York: Times Books, 1979), p. 188.

Two other observations must be made in concluding an analysis of the Carter Press Office. One is that the time of a total focus of attention on the Press Secretary is probably past. We found it necessary to discuss the Carter White House in terms of the work of Powell, Jagoda and Rafshoon. In Ford's time and also that of Nixon, others were involved in addition to the Press Secretary. So the Press Secretary remains the most prominent member of this group, but other functions beyond day-to-day media relations seem to be growing in importance. Still another factor brought out by Jagoda is that White House media advisers seem to beoome drawn into policy matters more than in the past.

An example of this was the refusal of the networks, late in 1979, to sell network prime time for the Carter-Mondale campaign. The reaction to this development by Powell and Rafshoon seemed to be that the networks, giving heavy coverage to such news events as the Kennedy Library dedication and the preliminaries of the Ted Kennedy announcement, seemed to turn a blind eye to the earlier starting time of campaigns. John Connally, while perhaps purchasing time from individual stations, was already using heavy media appeals for the Republican primaries. The FCC ruling favored the Carter-Mondale Committee; it was appealed to the courts.

Official White House Photograph

A veteran of Atlanta service, Jody Powell is widely considered to be quite authoritative as President Jimmy Carter's Press Secretary. Powell may be an example of the Policy Adviser type of Press Secretary.

CHAPTER SEVEN

BACKGROUND OF PRESS SECRETARIES (I)

Beginning with the assumption that the modern Press Secretary function really began with the Eisenhower Administration and James C. Hagerty, this chapter--which focuses on the pre-White House careers of Hagerty and Pierre Salinger, President Kennedy's Press Secretary--will include only the briefest summary of the men who held the title of Press Secretary between 1929 and 1953. These men were almost without exception former journalists who came directly into the White House from a newspaper or other journalistic career.

Stephen Early was acting as Press Secretary when Franklin D. Roosevelt held his first meeting with the White House Press. According to one account, Early took the small group from the Red Room upstairs to the President's study. Here FDR sat at a somewhat littered desk, shook hands with each journalist and read them a proclamation requiring a partial bank holiday.[1]

Early was still on the White House staff in April 1945 when he and Marvin McIntyre accompanied Mrs. Roosevelt to Warm Springs on the death of FDR.[2]

---

[1] Account of FDR's first press conference in Frank Freidel, _FDR: Launching the New Deal_ (Boston: Little, Brown, & Co., 1973), p. 216.

[2] James MacGregor Burns, _Roosevelt: The Soldier of Freedom, 1940-1945_ (New York: Harcourt, Brace, Jovanovich, 1970), p. 602. Early's expertise was acknowledged by several of his successors. See Chapter 15 reference in interview with Pierre Salinger.

Harry Truman was served by three Press Secretaries--Charles Ross, Joseph Short and Roger Tubby. All were competent men and each came from a journalistic background.

A long-time friend of Harry Truman, Charles G. Ross had been a Washington correspondent of the St. Louis Post-Dispatch. His journalistic achievements included recognition as a Pulitzer Prize winner.[3]

The death of Charles Ross prompted the appointment of Joseph Short, also a former journalist. Roger Tubby, the third of the Truman press aides, also later worked in political campaigns, as Pierre Salinger recalled in a Paris interview.

Up to this time, the Press Secretary was a technician, and he worked primarily with print media correspondents, although radio correspondents had been present at the White House as well. The technological breakthroughs of the 1950's coincided with James Hagerty's time in the White House. As George Christian noted in a 1978 interview, Hagerty basically set the pattern for modern media operations in the White House.

James Hagerty's Pre-White House Career-- James C. Hagerty came from a family in which a journalistic career had been if not a family tradition, at least a strongly felt influence. James Hagerty's father had been a political writer for the New York Times. In an oral history interview, Hagerty once stated that one of his earliest recollections was that of his father being at Sagamore Hill in Oyster Bay, Long Island, the home of President Theodore Roosevelt, on a trail of a

-----

[3]Patrick Anderson, The President's Men (Garden City, N.Y.: Doubleday & Co., 1968), p. 88. Anderson makes no reference to Short and Tubby, but the Truman Memoirs note that Short was serving when General McArthur was fired in 1951.

story of that period.

James C. Hagerty himself, prior to spending nearly 20 years in government service, first with Governor Thomas E. Dewey of New York and then with President Eisenhower, held several positions of responsibility in the print media. He had served as a political writer for the New York Times after graduating from Columbia University. He had been working as an Albany correspondent for the latter newspaper when he was pressed into service by Governor Dewey, who needed a principal aide for press relations.

Hagerty worked for Governor Dewey until the Governor permitted him to leave to work for General Dwight D. Eisenhower in the 1952 campaign After Eisenhower was elected, Hagerty served the full eight years of Eisenhower's term as the President's Press Secretary.

As a daily newspaper correspondent, Hagerty not only carried on the family tradition but he also gained experience which was extremely useful to him in working for Governor Dewey and President Eisenhower. One of the most necessary things in a Press Secretary's working relationship with all tha media is an ability to anticipate the needs of the working press. Since he had been a newspaperman for many years himself, this was quite possible and Hagerty was able to do this almost instinctively.

Hagerty's newspaper background, which was considerable, in addition to his reputation for outstanding competence and thoroughness, made him the nearest thing possible to a "journalist's journalist" and he had wide respect from the press corps in Washington.

Even those who might have been critical referred to him in a fashion indicating a respect for his professional expertise. For example, W. A. Swanberg commented in his study of the Henry Luce publishing organization:

" . . . The total effort of Eisenhower's press secretary, James Hagerty, . . . had been to shield the President, prevent the publication of any views or statements other than those of policy. . . . "[4]

One cogent analysis of Hagerty's service states:

"(Hagerty's) toughness, imagination, and zeal would soon make him the most effective--and, historically, the most important--of all the presidential Press Secretaries. Truman's Charlie Ross and Kennedy's Pierre Salinger were better liked, Roosevelt's Steve Early and Johnson's Bill Moyers had fuller understandings of public issues, but it was the tough-talking Irishman Jim Hagerty who would have the biggest impact on the delicate relationship between the President and the press.

"He was the first presidential Press Secretary to be, both by instinct and experience, more of a professional public-relations man than a newspaperman. The homely, stocky, chain-smoking, hard-drinking Hagerty looked and talked like a character out of The Front Page, but his instincts toward news manipulation and techniques of mass psychology were as smooth and sophisticated as any Madison Avenue executive. He had spent eight years as a political reporter for the New York Times, where his father, James A. Hagerty, was a longtime political writer. But in 1943, the thirty-four-year-old Hagerty quit the Times to accept a better-paying job as Governor Tom Dewey's press secretary. He said the move was only temporary,

---

[4]W.A. Swanberg, Luce and His Empire (New York: Dell Publishing Co., 1973), p. 611. The author was contrasting Hagerty's position with that of Emmet Hughes, author of The Ordeal of Power, a temporary consultant who Swanberg felt was more critical of Eisenhower than Hagerty had been.

but he had been with Dewey through nine years and two presidential campaigns when Dwight D. Eisenhower returned to the U.S. to run for President. Hagerty, having handled press relations for the Republican candidate of 1944 and 1948, was an obvious candidate to take over as Eisenhower's press chief.

"It was Hagerty's achievement, during his eight years as Press Secretary, to manage the news to an unprecedented degree, and still maintain the confidence and good will of the regular White House correspondents. The primary reason he was able to do this was his unsurpassed mastery of detail.

"Ninety percent of a Press Secretary's job is concerned not with policy but with endless routine: seeing that speeches and press releases are issued well in advance; arranging the press corps' travel plans on presidential trips; finding out what the President gave the First Lady for Christmas, and so forth. On such things Hagerty was unbeatable. A White House reporter compared him and Roosevelt's highly regarded Press Secretary, Steve Early, this way: 'Early could give you a long think-piece on the Administration's attitude toward the gold standard. Hagerty knows just what makes a good still picture, the exact amount of lighting needed for television, and exactly when to break up a press conference in order to make deadlines for home editions on the East Coast.'"[5]

A further comment on Hagerty's stewardship in the press office was made by Marquis Childs, the syndicated columnist:

"As legislative correspondent of the New York _Times_ in Albany at the age of twenty-nine,

---

[5]Patrick Anderson, The President's Men (Garden City, N.Y.: Doubleday & Co., 1968), pp. 181, 182.

Hagerty had attracted the attention of Governor
Dewey. In 1942, after eight years on the Times,
he joined Dewey's staff and quickly proved his
skill in dealing with the press. Twice for Dewey
and once for Eisenhower he went through the fear-
ful grind of a presidential campaign. In the White
House, as press secretary, he showed the same dex-
terity in a punishing job. His ability was in
holding the confidence of the regular White House
correspondents while at the same time keeping
them within the bounds of the news as he sought
to define it. Beyond that circle, as when he
ventured to brief the press at Bermuda and at the
summit, he was out of his depth. During the
President's illness he functioned with shrewd
skill . . ."[6]

In brief, Hagerty was widely admired for his
professional expertise. His great skill and the
President's confidence in him gave him a solid
reputation. This no doubt was enhanced by his
having grown up in an environment of political
journalism.

Pierre Salinger's Professional Background--
Pierre Salinger, the late President Kennedy's
Press Secretary, told this author that he felt a
solid background of journalistic experience was
invaluable to him in the Press Secretary's job.
He also detailed how his early interest in politics as a youth left its mark on his professional life and goals.

According to Salinger, "I was brought up in
a kind of political family, that was vitally interested in politics. They didn't, they weren't
politicians but they were interested in the issues
of their times and we talked politics around the
table. And I remember from a very young age that
I was fascinated by politics and that's why when
I got out of the Navy in 1946 I wanted to do some-

---

[6]Marquis Childs, Eisenhower: Captive Hero
(New York: Harcourt, Brace & Co., 1958), p. 220.

96

thing in the field of politics. I worked in the campaign for Mayor of San Francisco, and was involved in it off and on then until I worked in (the campaign of) 1960. I was very interested in it. We were also a family that was a very Democratic family, so I grew up in an atmosphere of Democratic thought, support for the Democratic party."[7]

As for his pre-White House experience, Salinger found certain aspects most helpful to him as Press Secretary. He commented," . . . I don't think you can be White House Press Secretary unless you've had extensive background in the press. And at the time I went to work for President Kennedy I'd had 14 years experience as a working journalist on the newspaper in San Francisco, the Chronicle, for a national magazine, Collier's magazine, and I think that experience was probably the most helpful of anything I'd had.

"Then, the second thing that qualified me was having had the experience of having gone through the campaign of Senator Kennedy. The campaign started with work in September (1959) and we started to make trips. In September '59 we started to make trips to various places; we would take a few reporters with us and gradually the number of reporters would increase until the day of the election we had 500 reporters covering our election headquarters in Hyannis Port, and then the rise of the press interest in the campaign came at the same time that I had a gradual (learning experience) and gained in my own knowledge of how to handle the job and be competent in it."[8]

Salinger noted that he had worked in the campaigns of Adlai Stevenson, who was Democratic

---

[7]Interview with Pierre Salinger, ABC News Bureau, 22 Avenue d'Eylau, Paris, September 18, 1979.

[8]Interview with Salinger in Paris, September 18, 1979.

presidential nominee in 1952 and 1956, and it was
actually an assignment for Collier's in 1956 to
cover an expose about the Teamsters Union which
brought him into contact first with Robert Kennedy,
counsel for the McClellan Subcommittee of the U.S.
Senate, and later with Senator John F. Kennedy
during the latter's Capitol Hill service.[9]

As White House Press Secretary, all accounts
this author has read plus his own contact with
Salinger indicate that it was not only Salinger's
professional competence, which was certainly com-
parable to that of Hagerty, which made him successful as Press Secretary. It was also his outgoing
personality and his skill in dealing with members
of the press that caused him to·rank among the
more skillful members of the select list of former
Press Secretaries.

Events with which Salinger had to deal
prior to the assassination included the Bay of
Pigs crisis, the Berlin crisis of 1961, the Cuban
missile crisis, and numerous domestic civil rights
crises including the Birmingham riots of 1963.
So it was an eventful if relatively brief era in
which Salinger served.

Some of his successors specifically noted
that they found him quite competent. Among these
was George Christian, the last of President Johnson's press secretaries.

In post-White House activities, Salinger has
remained active as a journalist. He published a
book entitled Je suis un americain (I Am an American) in 1975, according to Arthur Schlesinger

----

[9]See Salinger, With Kennedy (Garden City,
N.Y.: Doubleday & Co., 1966), pp. 13-28, for a
detailed description of this pre-White House
service. An account of the 1960 campaign is on
pp. 29-62.

Jr.[10] For several years, he was an American correspondent for the French publication L'Express.
After leaving L'Express in 1978, he joined ABC
News as a member of its Paris bureau, where he is
currently a European correspondent. A recent raid
on an IRA office in Dublin, where he was conducting an interview, indicates that he is still very
much an active newsman with the ability to follow
the important news.

----

[10]Interview with Arthur Schlesinger, Jr. in
Schlesinger's office, Graduate Center, City University of New York, July 1978.

CHAPTER EIGHT

BACKGROUND OF PRESS SECRETARIES (II)

The professional background and early careers of Lyndon Johnson's three press secretaries deserve close examination for clues to the kind of staff appointments made by President Johnson. Pierre Salinger served Johnson briefly, but he really belongs to the Kennedy Administration, and his credentials have been discussed in the previous chapter.

Therefore, our attention will be focused on George Reedy, Bill Moyers, and George Christian. Each of the three has written about his own experiences, although Moyers' book appears to be less of a memoir about the Johnson White House than reflections about the American political climate in the early 1970's.[1]

George Reedy had been on Lyndon Johnson's staff for some 13 years prior to the assassination and LBJ's sudden accession; at one time he had worked for a wire-service. In a correspondence with this author he denied vehemently that the Press Secretary is, or should be, the "President's man"; he indicated, and I am paraphrasing his words, that a press secretary should present the President's views and let the entire newsgathering process function as it will. I would identify him with the pre-"image" era, even though he carried

---

[1]See George Reedy, The Twilight of the Presidency (Cleveland: World, 1970), and The Presidency in Flux (New York: Columbia University Press, 1971); Bill Moyers, Listening to America (New York: Reader's Digest Press, 1971); George Christian, The President Steps Down (New York: Macmillan, 1970).

the title of Press Secretary.[2]

It would be worthwhile to return to Reedy's early life to determine how this master storyteller became the way he was when serving Lyndon Johnson.

It is known that when Reedy grew up in the Chicago area, he was a University of Chicago scholarship winner in the era of Robert M. Hutchins. In an interview with Arthur Schlesinger Jr., the author heard Reedy referred to as a very able man--a description used to refer to other members of the Johnson staff as well.[3]

Frank Cormier of the Associated Press recalls that at times Reedy would discuss with the White House correspondent corps various aspects of his early life. One recollection was that of an exchange with a reporter in which Reedy described how he played a trombone and a euphonium in the Senn High School band in Chicago between 1931 and 1934. At that time the band was the national championship band.[4]

Reedy was accustomed to excelling in what he did in his youth. He had worked for Johnson for

---

[2]Mr. Reedy told Seymour Hersh, New York Times correspondent, in a Gonzaga, Washington, symposium in 1977, that no one who has missed the experience of serving in the White House can possibly know anything realistic about the job of Press Secretary. Statements about correspondence are based on an exchange of letters in 1978.

[3]Interview with Arthur Schlesinger Jr., in Professor Schlesinger's office, Graduate Center, City University of New York, July 12, 1978.

[4]Frank Cormier, LBJ the Way He Was: A Personal Memoir of the Man and His Presidency (Garden City, NY: Doubleday & Co., 1977).

13 years prior to being named as LBJ's Press Secretary; as a journalist he previously had wire-service experience. Lillian Levy described him as unprepossessing, non-status seeking and absolutely honest. He was quoted by her as believing the Press Secretary's role was to provide "a source of accountable information" in a complex government.[5]

In _The Twilight of the Presidency_, Reedy expressed concern that Presidents become overinsulated from political reality and stated, "The monarchical character of the White House feeds such impulses and inhibits long-range thought."[6]

At a symposium in 1971 at Montauk, Long Island, Mr. Reedy commented: " . . . (T)he President doesn't have press problems; he has political problems and the press is the nearest thing he sees every day which brings his political problems home to him. I doubt whether the television media or, for that matter, the printed media are really consciously adopting the strategy: 'If I'm going to fight an invader, I'd like to fight as far away from home as possible.' . . ."[7]

It is difficult to determine why certain things occurred during Reedy's incumbency as Press Secretary, and whether these things can be linked to his early development. One episode was described by Marquis Childs:

"George Reedy suffered from a lack of confi-

---

[5]Lillian Levy, "A Source of Accountable Information", Washington _Star_ Sunday Magazine, March 7, 1965, quoted in Donald R. Burkholder, "The Caretakers of the Presidential Image", _Presidential Studies Quarterly_, Vol. V, No. 1, Winter 1975, pp. 38, 39.

[6]Reedy, _op. cit._, pp. 95-100.

[7]R. Gordon Hoxie, _The White House: Organization and Operations_ (New York: Center for the Study of the Presidency, 1971), p. 39.

dence on the part of his principal. Johnson had
a loudspeaker that piped Reedy's press conferences
into Johnson's private office. He (Johnson) monitored them. On occasion he would rush out into
Reedy's office to add his own comments. Poor
Reedy just suffered hell. . .

"Poor old Reedy was under terrible stress,
and had an illness with hammertoes, because he
was under terrible stress. That was an illustration of the importance of the lack of confidence
of the principal. . . ."[8]

Robert S. Allen, one-time collaborator with
Drew Pearson, found Johnson's media relations
wanting. He commented in part: ". . . There were
a lot of people here in (Washington) who weren't
particularly pro-Johnson. But they went out of
their way to cultivate these people. . . . It
could have been done more effectively and far more
astutely and successfully. One reason was Johnson's
exceedingly poor judgement in press secretaries.
George Reedy was brow-beaten and subservient, not
too bright to begin with. He treated George
atrociously, and George was at fault for allowing
himself to be treated that way. He should have
slammed him right back and told him to go to hell.
George finally reached a point where he couldn't
take it any longer, and quit. . . ."[9]

---

[8]Interview with Marquis Childs, United Feature
Syndicate/St. Louis Post-Dispatch at his office,
Post-Dispatch Washington Bureau, 1701 Pennsylvania
Avenue, N.W., October 27, 1978. See Chapter Three
for Reedy's view of this story.

[9]Oral History Interview with Robert S. Allen,
October 6, 1973, Lyndon Baines Johnson Library,
pp. 21-24, quoted in my "The Myth of the Johnson
'Credibility Gap'", Presidential Studies Quarterly,
forthcoming in 1980, with permission of PSQ.

Doris Kearns underlines one statement made by Reedy: "No White House assistant can stay in the President's graces for any considerable period without renouncing his own ego. . . . Those I have known who had kept some personality either left after a while or were careful to unleash their personality only in the President's absence."[10]

In considering Reedy's background as one who liked to excel and considering his feeling that a staff position requires the subordination of one's own ego, it appeared that he felt there was too much sycophantic behavior in the White House. One wonders why Reedy did not note such behavior on Senate staffs, but he apparently subscribed to the theory of the Imperial Presidency.

Could the service of Reedy at the White House, given the obvious recognition of his talent, have ended the way it did because of a personality conflict with LBJ, or are there some other possible explanations, such as a clash of the journalist's view of the Press Office function with that of an elected office-holder? There is some evidence that both Johnson and Nixon saw the media as an institution which should reflect official views only.

The only direct reference to Reedy in Johnson's official autobiography is an anecdotal account of how Reedy, Mrs. Johnson and others sought to persuade him (LBJ) not to step down by declining to seek re-election in 1964.[11]

Evans and Novak describe Reedy's departure from the White House: "On July 9, (1965), at the private urging of Mrs. Johnson, Moyers was named

---

[10]Doris Kearns, Lyndon Johnson and the American Dream (New York: Harper & Row, 1976), pp. 323, 324. Ms. Kearns quotes from Twilight of the Presidency.

[11]Lyndon Baines Johnson, The Vantage Point: Perspectives of the Presidency, 1963-1969 (New York: Holt, Rinehart & Winston, 1971), pp. 96-98.

press secretary to replace George Reedy, who longed
to leave the job and needed surgery to correct
a painful foot condition. It was a fundamental
change, not just of personnel but of basic function. For Moyers, retaining his role as Johnson's
policy staff chief, was to be no mere press aide
to the President. He would supplant the President in dealing with the press . . ." The columnists felt that Moyers shielded the Private Person
and only presented the Public Person to the media,
and that this improved Johnson's image for a time.[12]

Herbert Y. Schandler quotes Reedy, following
his departure from the White House, as being highly critical of Vietnam decision-making patterns.
Schandler states:

"Only faint echoes of the policy debate within the administration reached the American people
or, indeed, most of the government bureaucracy.
The President was insulated from the public, who
had the most at stake; his decisions were personal
decisions. 'The public's business--at the highest
level of life and death--was being determined as
though it were none of the public's business,'
Reedy has charged."[13]

In Reedy's pre-White House career, he served
on the staff of Senator Johnson on Capitol Hill.
Alfred Steinberg recalls how Reedy was pressed
into service when Majority Leader Johnson suffered
his heart attack in July 1955, but primarily dis-

---

[12]Rowland Evans and Robert Novak, Lyndon B.
Johnson: The Exercise of Power (New York: New
American Library, 1966), pp. 508-509.

[13]Herbert Y. Schandler, The Unmaking of a
President: Lyndon Johnson and Vietnam (Princeton, N.J.: Princeton University Press, 1977),
p. 329. Schandler quotes Reedy, "The Personal
Touch", New York Times, June 30, 1971.

cusses Reedy's White House service.[14]

Johnson's feelings toward Reedy appeared ambivalent, according to Richard Harwood and Haynes Johnson. They quoted LBJ as saying Reedy "carries more useless information around in his head than any man I knew. You can ask him about oatmeal and he will talk for hours." But later they said LBJ complained about reporters' treatment of Reedy, "picking at him, acting like he was a gladiator in an arena . . . George knows a lot more than Pierre (Salinger). George knows what he's talking about. Pierre just bulled it through. He announced a lot of things I never heard of."[15] Harwood and Johnson noted that "George Reedy, whom he once said was the man closest to him, left as press secretary and was disparaged."[16] Later, they noted, LBJ spoke the same way about Bill Moyers following Moyers' resignation.

From all evidence reflecting his views as published in two books and in his contributions to a Gonzaga symposium, Reedy felt the White House was a less congenial environment than the Senate for a leader such as Johnson. Doris Kearns explained that in the Senate, Johnson was obliged to negotiate and bargain with members of a peer group, while in the White House he was mostly surrounded by staff members whose careers depended largely on him.[17]

To get an idea of the kind of day that Reedy spent shortly after his boss had taken over as President and before he became Press Secretary, a

---

[14]Alfred Steinberg, Sam Johnson's Boy (New York: Macmillan, 1968), p. 415.

[15]Richard Harwood and Haynes Johnson, Lyndon, (New York: Praeger Publishers, 1973), p. 68.

[16]Harwood and Johnson, op. cit., p. 128.

[17]Kearns, op. cit., p. 323.

glimpse of his log indicates that on November 26, 1963, he had personal visits in his office from: Douglass Cater of the <u>Reporter</u> magazine; Larry Winship, publisher of the Boston <u>Globe</u>; Paul Miller, president of Gannett Newspapers; George Marder, UPI columnist; Paul Martin, Washington correspondent for Gannett; Stewart Alsop, <u>Saturday Evening Post</u>, for a luncheon visit; Ernest Barcella, of General Motors; Ira Capenstein, of the Post Office Department; Chuck Lipson, of the Retail Clerks; Tom Braden, publisher of the <u>Oceanside News</u> in California; Willard Shelton, of the <u>AFL-CIO News</u>, and Chuck Roberts and Bart Rowen, both of <u>Newsweek</u>.

On the same day, Reedy had telephone contacts with: Labor Secretary Willard Wirtz; George Meany, president of the AFL-CIO; J.C. Kellam of Station KTBC; John Lindsay of <u>Newsweek</u>; Cecil Holland of the Washington <u>Star</u>; Jim Akin of the Health, Education, and Welfare Department; Ernest Barcella of GM; Bart Rowan of <u>Newsweek</u>; a Mr. Spong of <u>Congressional Quarterly</u>; Gordon Chase of the National Security Council; Bill Anderson of the Sunday <u>Post</u> in Scotland; Bryan MacGee of Associated Rediffusion, Great Britain; Bill Stringham, <u>Christian Science Monitor</u>; Dan McCrary of <u>Business Week</u>; Marie Smith, Washington <u>Post</u>; Navy Secretary Ken Belieu; Jim Webb, NASA; Bob Baskin, Dallas <u>News</u>; Congressman Blatnik (D-Minnesota); Dwight Porter, Assistant Secretary of State; Congressman Powell (D-New York); Gordon Chase, National Security Council; Paul Martin, Gannett Newspapers; Blake Clark, <u>Reader's Digest</u>; Sam Brightman, Democratic National Committee; Jim Clardy, New York <u>Herald-Tribune</u>; Hobart Taylor, EEOC; Mr. Vohra, <u>Times of India</u>; Herb Kundic, Civil Defense; Eleanor Harris, <u>Ladies' Home Journal</u>; Phil Potter, Baltimore <u>Sun</u>, and Walter Cronkite, CBS.[18]

_____

[18]List compiled at Lyndon Baines Johnson Library, from Aides' Papers, Reedy Log for November 26, 1963, compiled August 1978.

After leaving the White House, in addition to his writing which resulted in two books, Reedy has had a distinguished career in Journalism education. He served as Dean of the Marquette University School of Journalism, Milwaukee.[19] He is now Nieman Professor at Marquette.

Bill Moyers' Professional Background--When George Reedy was obliged to leave the White House for health reasons, Bill Moyers added the duties of Press Secretary to his other staff responsibilities.

Moyers had become a member of the Johnson staff during the Senate years of LBJ's service. He first asked the Senator for a job during the 1954 "Firetruck" Dougherty campaign, according to Alfred Steinberg.[20]

After working in that campaign, Moyers completed his work at the University of Texas in Austin, while working at the Johnson radio and TV stations, KTBC. He then attended the University of Edinburgh for a year and spent two years at Southwestern Baptist Theological Seminary, after which he became an ordained minister.

But Steinberg writes that Moyers gave up his clerical career when Johnson offered him $10,000 to participate in his 1960 presidential campaign, and Moyers returned to politics. After a period of time as a vice presidential aide, Moyers entered the Peace Corps as a deputy director. On the day of the assassination, he was summoned to serve Johnson and never returned to the Peace Corps.

Steinberg comments of Moyers that he "was one

---

[19]William C. Spragens, The Presidency and the Mass Media in the Age of Television (Washington: University Press of America, 1978), p. 255.

[20]Alfred Steinberg, op. cit., p. 613.

of the few Johnson aides to escape the Presidential
bullyragging. Some said he did so because Johnson
knew the young man considered him with amusement,
an attitude he found baffling. However, Moyers
toiled long hours and possessed mature judgment,
even though he was only 29 years old. 'That boy
has a bleeding ulcer', Johnson spoke of Moyers
with pride to a visitor. 'He works for me like a
dog, and is just as faithful. He never asks for
anything--but for more work. He won't go hime with
that bleeding ulcer until nine or ten o'clock.
I don't know what I'd do without him.'"[21]

Theodore White writes that Moyers was an important aide who took over many of the chief of
staff duties when a scandal and poor health forced
Walter Jenkins, a veteran of the LBJ staff, to resign. Comments White on Moyers: "Bill Moyers, a
young man of 29, was as shy yet as important as
Sorensen had been; witty, thoughtful, of definitely
superior quality, he was, however, difficult to
get to and so dedicated to the President's privacy
that one could only vaguely guess where, in his
all-embracing functions, was the main thrust of
his influence. . . ."[22]

Moyers was described by one analyst as "a
very devoted Johnson staffer who had served in the
1964 campaign, then as chief of staff when Walter
Jenkins resigned. He also coordinated the Johnson
administration's historic 1965 legislative campaign. A young man with plenty of campaign experience and an ordained minister, his outgoing
personality stood him in good stead with the press
corps; he had little prior experience with the
news media. Moyers considered himself a 'very
pragmatic liberal', and he believed the White
House staff ought not to become public figures. .
. . (In a speech to a New York State editors

---

[21]Steinberg, op. cit., p. 633.

[22]Theodore H. White, The Making of the President 1964 (New York: Signet Books, 1966), p. 295.

110

group), Moyers commented in 1968 on the Presidency's credibility, as follows: (1) Some things are simply not suited for telling on the time schedule the inquisitive press prefers; (2) Events make lies out of the best promises. Circumstances change, and so must a President's strategy. His best intentions may be aborted as a result, and he may end up in public having said one thing and doing another. . . ."[23]

David Halberstam comments on Moyers' departure from the White House: ". . . The departure of Moyers in 1966 was considered crucial; though he had been the White House press officer and thus a spokesman for the war, he was known on the inside as a doubter, and he had worked to make other doubters available to the President. When Moyers left, feeling himself locked in by the growing inflexibility around him, James Reston wrote that he was a casuality of the war, that he had been wounded at Credibility Gap. Johnson himself was furious when Moyers left. . . ."[24]

What does this evidence indicate about Moyers' early political values and his goals and aims in becoming a part of the Johnson White House? The ministerial and Peace Corps experience indicate a strong public service orientation. His post-White house career has been in journalism, another profession in which he could serve in a different way.

---

[23]Donald R. Burkholder, "The Caretakers of the Presidential Image", Presidential Studies Quarterly, Winter 1975, Vol. V, No. 1, p. 39.

[24]David Halberstam, The Best and the Brightest (Greenwich, Conn.: Fawcett Crest Books, 1973), pp. 777, 778.

Upon leaving the White House, Moyers became editor of <u>Newsday</u>, the Long Island newspaper. After a few years serving there, he took a trip across the nation and his book previously referred to, <u>Listening to America</u>, was published. From this beginning of a journalistic career, he went to the Public Broadcasting Service, then to CBS and finally back to the PBS "Bill Moyers' Journal", which was his principal occupation at this writing.[25]

<u>George Christian's Professional Background</u>-- The last of Lyndon Johnson's Press Secretaries was a man who had come to the White House with experience as a press aide to two governors; in this sense George Christian's background resembled that of James C. Hagerty.

Christian, who had been press secretary for Governors Price Daniel and John Connally of Texas, came to the White House as an administrative assistant to the National Security Affairs adviser, Walt W. Rostow, in 1966. He stressed emphasizing the views of the President as accurately as possible; some felt as a technician he served Johnson better than any of the other aides, a view reflected in the Allen interview previously quoted.

As Burkholder notes, "Christian believed his primary duty as Press Secretary was to keep abreast of developments, both for his own background and in order to better understand and advise the President."[26]

---

[25] See Spragens, <u>The Presidency and the Mass Media in the Age of Television</u> (Washington: University Press of America, 1978), p. 255, for the views of George Christian, Moyers' successor as Press Secretary, about his departure from the White House.

[26] Burkholder, <u>op</u>. <u>cit</u>., p. 39.

Since it is reflective of the values he formed during his pre-White House career, some comments made by Mr. Christian during an interview in Austin are worth noting.

Of the Press Secretary, Christian said in 1978: "He's got a broader role today than existed at the time I was there. A Press Secretary can do more to report for reporters on things they're not privileged to be involved in. He ought to be their eyes and ears far more than he really is. But there is a time bind. A lot of what goes on in the White House ought to be reported, would be helpful to the President and put him in a proper perspective for the people. Almost everything the White House correspondents get, they're spoon fed. There's no reason for not giving them more. I used to question why a lot of things we were doing were not made public. Accounts of Presidential decision-making eventually get out. There's a lot more that could be made available that isn't. A lot of it remains totally private--falls between the cracks. There's very little danger of violating national security in most cases. Not enough attention is paid in the White House to making the decision-making process available to the press. There's too much fear you'll be misunderstood, and too much of an artificial air of decision-making. This situation has existed practically forever. The people don't look on a President as infallible--he's a man groping for answers to problems. When the public is not given a clear picture of the President and his problems, they have nothing on which to base confidence in him."[27]

Christian also commented, "I'm sure my experience with Governors Daniel and Connally helped me at the White House. This is partly why the press accepted me. They knew I was not totally

---

[27]Personal interview with George Christian in his office, American Bank Tower, Austin, Texas, August 28, 1978.

ignorant of executive politics. This was not always true of others, although it is doubtless true that James Hagerty's experience with Governor Dewey of New York helped him. This work for Daniel and Connally was a lot different in some ways but from the standpoint of preparation, I found an advantage of having been a statehouse Press Secretary. You're just working on a larger scale in Washington. My newspaper background was helpful; a Press Secretary ought to be able to see a reporter's point of view."[28]

Christian's White House experience prior to succeeding Moyers was as a second-echelon aide to Walt W. Rostow. He thus came to the job with White House experience as well as previous work as a statehouse Press Secretary.

To the extent that Christian was successful as Johnson's Press Secretary, it's likely that his depth of experience was helpful. He also shared the view of some of his successors that his principal function was to represent the President's views to the press and the various media without doing more than faithfully reflecting the President's thinking and his issue positions.

In his post-White House career, Mr. Christian has had a successful involvement in public relations work. He has his own public relations operation in Austin, which has been quite successful. His only recent involvement in national politics has been in acting as a consultant to the Democrats-for-Nixon campaign in 1972.

Summary of Background of LBJ's Press Secretaries--While Christian felt that both Reedy and Moyers were more articulate than he, and he excelled in the written word, each came from a background which strongly reflected their political

_____

[28]Christian interview, August 28, 1978, cited on page 49.

interests and their verbal skills.

The ideological background of these men appeared to have less impact on their successful service than their ability to reflect the President's views accurately. They worked for a demanding President, but each performed his work well when he was given the freedom to do so.

CHAPTER NINE

BACKGROUND OF PRESS SECRETARIES (III)

The Nixon Administration worked with a
regularly appointed Press Secretary, Ron Ziegler,
and in its final months with an acting Press
Secretary, Gerald Warren. Besides these individuals in the Nixon White House, a Communications
Director functioned there, with three persons
holding that assignment. These were Herb Klein,
a long-time associate of Richard Nixon who was
his press aide when he was vice president; Ken
Clawson who held this position for a time, and
finally Ziegler who received the Communications
Director assignment in the final part of the
Nixon Administration.

Some of the early background of these staff
people will be considered in this chapter.

Ron Ziegler's Professional Background--Ronald
L. Ziegler came to the Nixon staff in the 1968
presidential campaign from a position with the
J. Walter Thompson advertising agency as an account
executive.[1] He was 30 at the beginning of
Nixon's first term. Ziegler had as an employee
of the Thompson organization had business contacts with H. R. Haldeman, who became one of
the two principal Nixon aides.

One common bit of talk around Washington by
Nixon critics during the first Nixon term was
that Ziegler, a Louisville native, had begun his

----

[1]See William Safire, Before the Fall: An
Inside View of the Pre-Watergate White House
(New York: Belmont Tower Books, 1975), p. 125.

career as a salesman of riverboat-ride tickets at Disneyland in California, before joining the Thompson agency. The implication was that he was a shameless huckster.

A different view was presented by William Safire who commented:

"A word here about Ziegler. In 1972 a network bureau chief in Washington, pledging me to darkest secrecy, said he thought Ziegler was the most effective Presidential press secretary since Jim Hagerty, and probably better at the care and feeding of the press on trips than Hagerty. His praise for Ziegler had to be anonymous because it would have seemed like snuggling up to the White House, a position no self-respecting journalist would ever allow himself to assume. Most of the press corps began by treating Ziegler like a puppy-dog front man, recognizing his advertising background and low rating in the inner circle to be the insult it really was; then, as he grew in stature in the White House inner circle, and his ability to fend off their questions gained some finesse, they began to see him as the symbol of their frustrations. Though journalists are quick to point out that 'it is unfair to blame the messenger for the bad news', many angrily blamed messenger Ziegler for the lack of news or the manipulation of the news, often forgetting that his role was to be more the President's press secretary than the press's representative to the President.

"Ron was a better reporter than some reporters. Before an 11 a.m. briefing, he would study the papers and the wires, and call around the White House and the agencies of government, not only to find out what he could say but what he could not say. Learning when to stop is a skill underestimated by most of his interlocutors. He has a necessary sense of humor (his imitation of comedian David Frye imitating the President, eyes rolling upward and fingers wiggling the 'V' sign, is hilarious); an unnecessary streak of cruelty that probably comes from contemptuous treatment by Haldeman at staff meetings as a mouth and not a mind; a blotter-like memory that can absorb a briefing and play it back in more coherent form; and an unfortunate inclination to use the language of the computer. . . .

"The job he held for more than four years is harder than almost any other job in government: the fury with which the press corps sometimes goes after the press secretary dismays some of the White House regulars themselves. One Saturday morning, when there was no briefing, I was in the Health Unit, the combination sauna-shower-exercise room Haldeman had built in the basement of the EOB. Ziegler was showering; something went wrong with the plumbing, and the water turned first scalding hot and then freezing cold; Ziegler in his panic couldn't get the door to the shower stall open and took the full fury of the crazed plumbing. When he got out, the press secretary sat huddled in a towel for ten minutes, skin red and teeth chattering, and all he could say was, 'Jesus, it was just like the daily briefing.' . . . "[2]

Theodore White, in describing the 1972 campaign for the Presidency, disclosed his view of Ziegler's background:

" . . . In 1960 there had been one Disneyland, in Anaheim, California; by 1972 it had received over 100,000,000 visitors--and its cheerful young public-relations officer, Ronald Ziegler, had graduated to become the stern public spokesman of Richard Nixon. . . ."[3]

---

[2]Safire, op. cit., pp. 351-352.

[3]Theodore H. White, The Making of the President 1972 (New York: Bantam Books, 1973), p. 207.

Concerning the latter period of the Nixon Administration, White has written of Ziegler:

"The White House press room, which had become a bear pit over the previous two years--with Ziegler the bear to be baited--now reached a state of macabre sadism and black humor. Ziegler became more than ever elusive, and more and more often his deputy Gerald Warren filled in. 'Can you tell us, Jerry, when we might expect a news conference or when the President plans to answer any questions in any form about some of these very serious charges of corruption?' Warren: 'I have nothing to offer you on any of these subjects.' Or--Q: 'Are you aware of any new instructions going out to government public-relations officials on how to handle the press?' A: 'I would welcome some myself.' Was it true, one reporter asked of Warren, that the President would not hold another press conference until White House reporters stopped shouting at Ron Ziegler? 'I think it would be nice if they did', replied the mild-mannered Warren. Q: 'Would it be nice if we stopped shouting at you?' Warren: 'You don't shout at me.' Q: 'I wonder if we could have a show of hands of people willing not to shout at the President if he would hold a press conference?' Warren: 'I would be willing to accept the show of hands, too.'

"In June, the National Press Club, long past its days as a vital institution, shot off what was, for it, a blast of enormous daring. A committee headed by James McCartney of the Knight newspapers condemned Ziegler publicly: 'The White House press secretary has been reduced to a totally programmed spokesman without independent authority or comprehensive background or knowledge of Administration policies. Rather than opening a window into the White House, the press secretary closes doors. Information about public business is supplied on a selective, self-serving basis.

Legitimate questions about public affairs are not answered on a day-to-day basis; even worse, such questions are often not seriously considered.' The nation was full of questions; nothing made sense; it was a time of chaos."[4]

Raymond Price, a Nixon speechwriter, describes his weekend spent with Ziegler at Camp David before the President announced the resignation of Haldeman and Ehrlichman:

"Throughout the weekend, Ziegler and I repeatedly interrupted our work to review the arguments and worry through the question, over coffee during the day or over a double scotch in the evening; Was this the right course? Did Bob and John have to go? In this, Ron was reflecting Nixon's own doubts, his own reluctance, his own pain. Intellectually, Nixon had concluded--with less than 100-percent certainty, but with more than 50-percent certainty--that it had to be done. Emotionally, he was wracked by the doing of it. Ron, in turn, was wracked by having to advise the President that it was necessary. Before joining the campaign in 1968 Ron had worked for Haldeman in the Los Angeles office of the J. Walter Thompson Advertising Agency--a job Haldeman gave him after Ron had worked under Haldeman in Nixon's 1962 gubernatorial campaign. Then Bob had brought Ron into the 1968 campaign. Each time we debated it, however, we came to the same reluctant conclusion: Yes, it had to be done."[5]

J. Anthony Lukas referred to Ziegler during the Watergate period in this vein:

---

[4]Theodore H. White, Breach of Faith--The Fall of Richard Nixon (New York: Dell Books, 1975), pp. 312-313.

[5]Raymond Price, With Nixon (New York: Viking Press, 1977), pp. 99-100.

(In New Orleans at the VFW convention)
"(p)erhaps the most revealing incident of the
day occurred just before (the President) entered
the convention hall. As Ron Ziegler and the
White House press corps trooped after him, Nixon
abruptly grabbed Ziegler by the shoulders and
shoved him towards the reporters, saying, 'I
don't want any press with me. You take care of
it.'

"The President's shove was but the latest
indignity heaped on the husky shoulders of the
former fullback from Dixie Heights High. Melvin
Laird and John Connally had both called for his
dismissal. A committee of the staid National
Press Club had declared that Ronald Ziegler
'misled the public and affronted the professional
standards of the Washington press corps.' And
White House reporters had been griping for years
about his talents for obfuscation (he quickly
was nicknamed 'Zigzag' and his answers labeled
'Ziegles'). They pointed to classics such as
his reply when asked whether allied troops were
preparing to invade Laos: 'The President is
aware of what is going on in Southeast Asia.
That is not to say that anything is going on in
Southeast Asia.' Or his response when pressed to
explain what he meant by the President's 'least
unlikely' decision: 'You should not interpret
by my use of "least unlikely" that ultimately,
or when the final decision is made, that that
may not be the decision, but what I'm saying is
that it is only one of the matters under consideration and the decision has not been made.' But
the reporters' irritation escalated to indignation
over Ziegler's bluff stonewalling on Watergate,
a subject on which he seemed to follow the
maxim, 'When in doubt deny everything.' But
probably nothing brought more scorn down on
Ziegler's head than his acceptance of a reporter's
phrasing on April 17, 1973. After Nixon announced
'major developments' in the Watergate case that
day, Ziegler told reporters that this was the
President's 'operative' statement. R. W. Apple

of the New York _Times_ asked whether that meant
'that the other statement is no longer operative,
that it is now inoperative.' After fencing with
Apple for a while, Ziegler finally gave in: 'The
President refers to the fact that there is new
material; therefore this is the operative statement. The others are inoperative.' The next day
Clark Mollenhoff of the Des Moines _Register_, a
former Presidential assistant who felt burned by
his very association with Nixon, thundered at
Ziegler: 'Do you feel free to stand up there and
lie and put out misinformation and then come around
later and say it's all "inoperative"? That's
what you're doing. You're not entitled to any
credibility at all.' Relations between Ziegler
and the press became so embittered that White
House officials declined to appear in the White
House press room, calling it a 'poisoned forum.'
Even a gracious apology to Woodstein--whose stories
he had once labeled 'shabby journalism'--did not
earn Ziegler any good will. So gradually he
relinquished the briefings to Assistant Press
Secretary Gerald L. Warren (a former newsman) and
went on to more majestic matters. Part of
Ziegler's problem with the press was that he had
never been a reporter. Growing up in Covington,
Kentucky, he became a star running back in high
school, where his kindergarten sweetheart (and
future wife) was the football queen and led
Z-I-E-G-L-E-R cheers for him. He won a football
scholarship to Xavier University in Cincinnati,
but soon followed the sun west to Los Angeles,
where he got a job for the summer piloting the
'jungle cruise boat' at Disneyland and giving the
same spiel thirty-three times a day: 'Welcome
aboard, folks. My name's Ron. I'm your skipper
and guide down the River of Adventure. Before we
pull away from the dock, please turn around and
take a good look. You may never see it again . . .
On the left, the natives on the bank. The natives
have only one aim in life and that is to get
a-head.' He liked California so much that he

transferred to USC, where he was a B- marketing
major, Sigma Chi social chairman, and active Young
Republican. When Nixon came to USC in 1960 for
a campaign speech, Ziegler handled press arrangements for the visit. He worked in the disastrous
1962 campaign, but impressed the campaign manager,
Bob Haldeman, who recruited him for J. Walter
Thompson. In his five years there, Ziegler became
an account executive for Disneyland, Sea World,
7-Up, and Blue Chip Stamps. Haldeman took him
into the 1968 Presidential campaign and then into
the White House, where he first held the lowly
title of 'press assistant.' Later he got the
full 'press secretary' title, and when Haldeman,
Ehrlichman, Colson, et. al., left the White House
in the spring of 1973, Ziegler suddenly found
himself Nixon's last link to a lost past. On
June 6 the President gave him complete responsibility for all White House communications matters
and the additional title of assistant to the
President. As summer wore on, Ziegler joined Haig
and Kissinger in the new 'inner circle' of advisers.
Nobody knew what Ziegler advised the President on.
'He doesn't know anything about PR,' said one
aide. 'So it must be PR.'"[6]

Unlike some of his White House associates,
Ziegler has declined to write a book up to the
early 1980's. He has given an interview to Dom
Bonafede, referred to in an earlier chapter. He
also appeared in two symposia featuring former
Press Secretaries, one at the University of Texas
in Austin and one at Gonzaga University in
Spokane.

Other participants in the Austin symposium
besides Ziegler and Gerald Warren included Liz

---

[6]J. Anthony Lukas, Nightmare: The Underside
of the Nixon Years (New York: Viking Press, 1976),
pp. 429-431.

Carpenter, George Christian, Frank Cormier of the Associated Press, James Deakin of the St. Louis Post-Dispatch, W. Thomas Johnson, Herbert G. Klein, Joseph Laitin, Marianne Means, Ronald H. Nessen, Dan Rather, Hugh Sidey, Jerald F. terHorst, Helen Thomas of United Press International, and William S. White. Some excerpts from the comments of Ziegler:

" . . . (Y)ou have to keep in mind that I uttered the phrase 'inoperative,' so, in order to address this question with credibility (whether or not Ziegler was ever asked to evade the truth) let's put that on the table.

"I agree with my two former colleagues who say that the press secretary is only as good as the information he is given. I can underline that many, many times, in referring to certain aspects of the Nixon years.

"With that aside, obviously things that were said in terms of Watergate turned out to be untrue and we all know that. I will say, however, that--and I think all of us would be honest; I know I am being--in terms of major policy and major events that affect the country, I can say that I was never asked to go out before the press corps and tell a lie.

"Now, there are times when a press secretary is faced with and the President of the United States is faced with a situation where you cannot speak or cannot get into an issue and should not get into an issue, and that happens often. However, press secretaries do find themselves in a situation where they do in fact lie because of the infor- mation that one of their colleagues gave them, which they felt to be true, and that ends up not to be true. So that is a dilemma that a press secretary faces. Some have had to deal with it in a far more serious way than others.

"I would add one point. In Dan Rather's
reference to the propaganda podium or propaganda
pulpit, and also what Tom Johnson said--one of the
problems a press secretary in modern times faces,
in my view, is that you have to brief every day.
There are a 100--between 80 and 115 reporters--in
that room every day. And a press secretary stands
before them and has to answer questions covering
foreign policy, domestic policy, the attitude of
the President, the position of the President on a
number of issues, and he has to do it to the best
of his ability in a truthful, straightforward
way. But it is impossible, in my opinion, for
one man today to be briefed, to have the insight
into all of these issues, and do a kind of job
that is adequate . . .

"I know when I was in the White House and we
went through a period where a number of press
conferences were not being held, I used to look
back on the days of President Kennedy and say to
myself, 'My God, wouldn't it be wonderful if the
President would have a press conference every
week. My job would be, a cakewalk.' Because
I'd be in a position that all I would have to say
is that, 'The President will address that subject
in his Friday press conference.'

"But I do think a solution has to be found to
the increasing demands that fall on the man called
the press secretary. I do not know if it is
establishing two press secretaries who have equal
stature and equal access to the President. I do
not know if it is establishing a foreign policy
press secretary to complement what the President's
press secretary would do who deals with domestic
and basic daily Presidential affairs, but somehow,
a solution, I think, has to be found.

"I do believe there is some movement to this
type of consideration. We tried to do it a little
bit in the last year but we became diverted. I

think Mr. Nessen is probably trying to move somewhat in that direction at this time."[7]

At the Gonzaga symposium, Ziegler admitted
to having been misled by his President but
declined to criticize his former boss because of
this. He commented, in part:

" . . . (M)uch of the information that I gave
about Watergate at some point turned out to be
incorrect. That is an understatement to say the
least. It is something that has troubled me a
great deal because much of the information, and
I think this goes to the heart of your questions
. . . that I gave as press secretary about Watergate was incorrect because I was not told what
the facts were--to answer your question. And in
fact historically I think it has been shown that
I was a part or a victim (to use that word) of
the Watergate coverup which did take place. Have
I learned anything from it? I have learned that
anyone who holds the position as press secretary
or spokesman must be aware that the information
that he provides is only as good as what he is
able to find out or is told. I suppose when I
look back on it I didn't find out enough and
perhaps myself did not probe the issue to its
greatest extent as possible from the inside; and
the result I think is history . . . .

" . . . I don't feel that anything would be
served by publicly criticizing anyone. Former
President Nixon is still a friend of mine. I
have a great respect for him. I can understand
his weak side and his strengths. Certainly
there is no one in this room, including myself,
who knows that President Nixon did not make

---

[7]Hoyt Purvis, ed., The Presidency and the
Press (Austin, Texas: Lyndon Baines Johnson
School of Public Affairs, 1976), pp. 36-37.

serious mistakes in the way the entire Watergate
episode was dealt with. I can say that freely
and without any concern that would infringe upon
my friendship for him or my respect of him. In
short, he blew the Watergate matter. And, I
think he knows that."[8]

From the various sources cited, it becomes
obvious that Ziegler had a quite circumscribed
role as White House press secretary. This of
course did have the advantage for him of keeping
him out of some of the difficulties that his
associates encountered.

Ziegler's reassignment as communications
director occurred after Herb Klein's departure
from the White House at the end of the first
Nixon term. The responsibilities of this
position have previously been described.

After Nixon's resignation, Ziegler served
for a time on the ex-President's San Clemente
staff prior to the decision in 1979 by Richard
Nixon that he would return to New York.

After leaving Mr. Nixon's employ, Ziegler
entered a post-White House career in the engineering business. He was associated with a firm in the
East at this writing.

Gerald Warren's Professional Background--
Gerald L. Warren, who became acting Press
Secretary for President Nixon when Ziegler moved
to the Communications Director's position, had
been a print journalist prior to his White House
experience.

---

[8]The Presidential Press Secretaries Forum:
April 1, 1978, Campus of Gonzaga University,
p. 13.

His tenure as White House press secretary was a relatively brief one, since the Nixon resignation cut it short. He essentially took over from Ziegler after relations between Ziegler and the White House press corps had become quite difficult.

Warren has returned to a journalistic career, but he did come into the limelight briefly as moderator of the Austin symposium on press secretaries held in 1976 and referred to previously.

In this capacity, Warren recalled a comment made by Mrs. Lyndon Johnson about Mrs. Gerald Ford, as follows: "She said that anyone who has lived in . . . the White House, has a certain respect for and understanding for those who live there now.

"I think that is also true for anyone who has worked there, and particularly in the position that these gentlemen held, with the daily focus of attention. There is an understanding. There is an affinity. . . ."[9]

Communications Directors: Herb Klein, Ken Clawson, and Ron Ziegler--Although the Nixon White House originated the concept of communications director in the White House, this position is not to be confused with that of director of the Office of Telecommunications Policy held by Clay Whitehead during the Nixon era. Whitehead's job was to attempt to develop long-term policy initiatives to supplement the work of the Federal Communications Commission.

The communications director had a more generalized task than the press secretary, who was in charge of day-to-day media relations. To some extent, Klein pioneered the development of White House contacts with the media outside Washington,

---

[9] Hoyt Purvis, ed., op. cit., p. 22.

as indicated by this comment he made at the Austin symposium:

"I think that there is a role for both the White House press corps and the press outside Washington. In fact, that is what Helen (Thomas of the UPI) is saying. There is certainly a role for the White House press corps in questioning both the press secretaries and the President.

"I found when I went into office that no one had really paid attention to the press outside of Washington. And there is a basic difference. People in Texas have different questions than those in Washington because they look at things in a different perspective. The same could be said for Los Angeles or Chicago. . . .

" I have always believed that one of the best ways that a President or a cabinet official has of knowing what is going on is by listening to what kind of questions he gets. I think there is a real need for the questions in Washington, but certainly there is a great value in having questions from other areas too.

"And the quality of reporting, I think, has gone up all around the country. I am not sure that the quality of questions has. Too often, both in Washington and some of the other areas, reporters today--particularly when the television camera is on--are too prone to make statements rather than ask questions. That is something that needs to be examined.

"Another matter I want to mention is the follow-up question. I think the follow-up question is excellent and it has been developed more in the Ford Administration.

"Sometimes because there has been so much work on a question, I think that someone could ask the President, 'Are we going to invade Cuba tomorrow and the President would say, 'Yes.' And yet because the next questioner had been waiting with his rehearsed question, he would say, 'Now about the welfare problem.' There is not enough flexibility in how it is handled.

"One other thing I would say on this subject of 'going around the White House press corps.' I do not consider it that. I think there is a need to have the President learn by what is asked of him outside. That is not going around. I think that is part of the education, part of keeping the President in contact with the real world, not only in Washington and New York, but in Austin, and in Chicago, and Los Angeles."[10]

Herb Klein, a one-time reporter and editor of the San Diego Union, joined Richard Nixon early in his political career. This long-time newsman served Nixon as press secretary during the Senate and Vice Presidency. He was also press secretary during the two earliest Nixon presidential campaigns (1960 and 1968) and during the ill-fated California gubernatorial campaign (1962). Klein served in the Nixon White House through the first term, but he left in 1973 to return to a career in journalism.

Ken Clawson was brought in to replace Klein after the latter's resignation from the White House staff. Clawson has a background as a newspaperman. He had been on the staff of the Toledo Blade at one time. Two references are made to him by Raymond Price, the Nixon speechwriter. One is to the release of a statement by Clawson as communications director maintaining that Charles Colson, a resigned Nixon aide, "was being sentenced for a felony that had been 'standard practice of members and staff of the Senate Watergate committee for more than a year and the same felony being committed

---

[10]Hoyt Purvis, ed., op. cit., pp. 26-27.

131

daily by some partisan members of the House
Judiciary Committee.'"[11]

The second reference to Clawson in Price's
memoirs details a series of strategy meetings with
White House Chief of Staff Alexander Haig in 1974.
Besides the communications director, according to
Price, the strategy group included Ron Ziegler,
General Haig, Dean Burch (former FCC chairman),
James St. Clair (the President's attorney), J. Fred
Buzhardt Jr., and William Timmons. As a result
of health problems, Clawson left the staff and was
succeeded in the final months of Nixon's tenure by
Ziegler who has been discussed in detail earlier
in this chapter.[12]

Although Ziegler's tenure was brief as
communications director, he found in it a respite
from the exacerbated daily contact with the
Washington correspondent corps. Ziegler thus had
served as a press aide in Nixon campaigns for public
office, as a press assistant early in the first
Nixon term, during most of Nixon's term as Press
Secretary, and in these final months prior to the
resignation as communications director.

After Nixon went into retirement at San
Clemente, Ziegler worked on his staff there for
a time. By the period of the 1977 David Frost
interviews with the former President, Ziegler had
struck out on his own. But as he noted in the
Gonzaga symposium, he still refused to criticize
his former chief, even though admitting that
much information was withheld from him during the
Watergate period.

---

[11]Raymond Price, op. cit., p. 294.

[12]Price, op. cit., p. 323.

Near the end of Ziegler's tenure as Press
Secretary, he did issue a public apology to the
Washington _Post_ which published the earliest
Watergate stories.[13]

———————

[13]Carl Bernstein and Bob Woodward, _All the
President's Men_ (New York: Simon and Schuster,
1974), p. 311.

CHAPTER TEN

BACKGROUND OF PRESS SECRETARIES (IV)

Gerald R. Ford's Press Secretaries (1974-1977)--
During the White House period of Gerald R. Ford,
somewhat less attention was paid to the communications director's role than was true with either
Nixon or Carter, so the focus of attention in
this chapter will be on the two Press Secretaries,
Jerald terHorst and Ronald Nessen.

President Ford quickly downgraded the Office
of Telecommunications Policy within the White House,
which had been headed by Clay T. Whitehead under
President Nixon; Ford was more concerned with
public contact and sought to avoid aloofness; his
action in downgrading OTP foreshadowed the action
of President Carter shifting this function back
into the Department of Commerce.

The tenure of Jerald terHorst at the White
House was brief and it ended with a dispute between
terHorst and other Ford staff members about the
Press Secretary's being kept in the dark about
the Nixon pardon.

After terHorst's departure from the White
House in September 1974, Ron Nessen became his
successor and was the principal figure in the media
relations of the Ford White House until the end
of President Ford's term in 1977.

Jerald terHorst's Professional Background--
Jerald terHorst came to his appointment as President
Ford's first Press Secretary from a background of
long experience as a Washington and foreign correspondent for the Detroit News. He had known the
former House Minority Leader since Ford's first
election to Congress in 1946, but in the pre-White

House period Ford's Press Secretary had been Paul Miltich.[1]

Miltich had been assisted by John W. (Bill) Roberts, who had a broadcasting background with the _Time-Life_ organization.[2]

With Gerald Ford's accession to the Presidency in August 1974, however, the new President sought a Press Secretary who had much credibility with the Washington correspondent corps.

He found this choice through the selection of Jerald F. terHorst, who in 1974 was serving as chief of the Washington Bureau of the Detroit _News_.

TerHorst, a native of Michigan, had served 16 years in Washington and overseas as a correspondent for the _News_. After his brief service with Ford, he returned to that assignment and was continuing to hold it at this writing. He was an object of much controversy after his resignation over the Nixon pardon, but a look at his early career and comments made about him by other persons may shed some light on the nature of his personality and character which prompted him to take this unusual action.

Resignations of this type are a deviation from the norm in American politics, according to two authors who cite the resignation of Attorney General Elliot Richardson and his principal assistant, William D. Ruckleshaus, as unusual. This did, of course, set a pattern of deviation for the

---

[1]See Bud Vestal, _Jerry Ford Up Close_ (New York: Berkley Medallion Books, 1974), p. 37. Miltich served Ford in the House and also during his term as Vice President.

[2]Vestal, _op. cit._, pp. 37-38.

terHorst resignation.[3]

According to Mr. terHorst's publishers, The Third Press of New York, this journalist had filed stories from Europe, Asia, the Middle East and Latin America. He had covered such stories in his newspaper career as the Berlin Crisis of 1961 and various phases of the Middle Eastern conflict.

Prior to taking the White House appointment, he had been writing a syndicated column which appeared in approximately 100 major American daily newspapers. Since 1960 he covered every major presidential trip both abroad and in the United States; these assignments included the Nixon summit visits to the Soviet Union and People's Republic of China.

During terHorst's early career in Grand Rapids, he became a friend of Ford's although the pardon incident appears to have ruptured that friendship permanently, despite Ford's lack of reputation for being vindictive.

During World War II, after beginning his journalistic career in Grand Rapids, terHorst served as a U.S. Marine Corps officer and again during the Korean War returned to active service. He benefited by comparison with Ron Ziegler, his immediate predecessor who had a difficult relation with the news media and lost respect because of not being taken into Nixon's confidence.

---

[3]Edward Weisband and Thomas M. Franck, Resignation in Protest (New York: Penguin Books, 1976), pp. 13-14. These authors give an account of the "Saturday night massacre" in which Richardson and Ruckleshaus had forced resignations rather than be a party to a breach of the former's word to Congress.

Comments from Washington journalists suggest this. David Brinkley of NBC News stated the he was "one who admired Jerry terHorst before he resigned as White House Press Secretary, and more so since he did", and Tom Wicker of the New York Times praised terHorst's account of Ford's pre-White House career. Mary McGrory of the Washington Star referred to terHorst as "the man who served (Ford) so admirably and briefly as Press Secretary", and David Broder in commenting on the terHorst book about Ford said terHorst "has told almost everything there is to tell about President Ford at this point . . ."[4]

Nonetheless, many Nixon loyalists took offense at terHorst's resignation and expressed bitterness about it.

One comment made about the resignation by President Ford was reported by John Osborne, long-time White House observer, who stated:

"Mr. Ford's Press Secretary and friend of 25 years, Jerry terHorst, resigned in protest (of the pardon). A matter of principle, he said. He is suspected at the White House of wanting out anyhow and of using the pardon as a pretext. Mr. Ford believed it was indeed an act of principle. 'You just don't understand these evangelical Michigan Dutchmen,' he told an outraged loyalist."[5]

---

[4]Publisher's and journalists' comments about terHorst on jacket of Jerald terHorst, Gerald Ford and the Future of the Presidency (New York: Third Press, 1974).

[5]John Osborne, White House Watch: The Ford Years (Washington: New Republic Books, 1977), p. 7.

In his memoirs, former President Ford told how terHorst suggested moving reporters' chairs closer to the podium for presidential news conferences, removing the Nixon blue curtain and placing the President in front of a symbolic open door to the East Room.[6]

In general, terHorst maintained his professional standing with the Washington correspondent corps. But it came at the cost of much criticism from the Ford staff on which he had served so briefly. The former President's comment reported by Osborne indicates that the early values instilled in terHorst in his Dutch Reformed environment in Grand Rapids played a major part in his behavior at the time of the resignation.

Ron Nessen's Professional Background--Somewhat better known as Ford's Press Secretary because of his longer service with the Ford White House, Ronald Nessen came from a different background than that of terHorst--Nessen had been a broadcast correspondent, most recently with NBC News at the time of his appointment. In Ford's account he indicates terHorst's staff probably lacked sufficient background to take over full responsibilities as Press Secretary; he also indicates he clarified with Nessen that the latter was not likely to "go public" with a resignation statement in the event of another such controversial action as Ford's pardon of Nixon.[7]

Nessen's account of his service under Ford indicates that his first decisions as Press Secretary had to do with decisions about what to do with

---

[6]Gerald R. Ford, A Time to Heal (New York: Harper & Row/Reader's Digest, 1979), pp. 156-157.

[7]Gerald R. Ford, op. cit., p. 184.

the White House Press Office staff. One person
who was retained was Gerald Warren, who had been
acting Press Secretary at the end of the Nixon
period. Kenneth Clawson, former Washington <u>Post</u>
reporter who had been communications director for
a time, and Father John McLaughlin, a vociferous
Nixon defender during the Watergate period, were
among those Nessen decided not to retain in the
communications operation. Nessen also indicates
some left-over bitterness from the Nixon period
despite the effort to improve White House media
relations.[8]

Nessen had served 20 years as a journalist,
but he felt at the time of his White House appointment that his NBC assignment was insufficiently
challenging with "the need to cram the most
complex subjects into 100 or 150 words".[9]

Osborne recalls Nessen's first White House
briefing as follows:

"In the seventh week of Gerald Ford's
Presidency his second press secretary and third
spokesman--a deputy press secretary filled the gap
between the first and second unfortunates who
held the full title--thought it necessary to say
to White House reporters: "It's a Ford White House
now and it's not a Nixon White House.'

"This was beginning to be true but it still
was not entirely true when Ronald H. (Ron) Nessen,
aged 40, a former UPI and NBC correspondent, said
it at his first briefing in the White House press
room on September 24. Four days, a weekend and a
speaking trip to Detroit had intervened since Mr.

---

[8]Ron Nessen, <u>It Sure Looks Different from the
Inside</u> (Chicago: Playboy Press, 1978), pp. 30-32.

[9]Nessen, <u>op. cit.</u>, pp. 11-12.

Ford, obviously embarrassed, had introduced Nessen
to the White House press corps as the successor
to the President's first press secretary and friend
of a quarter century, Jerry terHorst, who quit in
protest against the Nixon pardon just before it was
announced on September 8. In different words but
in much the same way that terHorst had done,
Nessen had gone through the ritual at his introduction on September 28 of saying that 'I will never
knowingly lie to the White House press corps' and
'I will never knowingly mislead the White House
press corps.' 'Lie' may be too strong a term for
what all official spokesmen have to do at times.
But Nessen presumably knew that he would be misleading the press by omission if not by explicit
statement now and again.

"Doubters are invited to compare the impression
of a smooth and friendly transition that terHorst
conveyed during his 30 days as press secretary with
his account in the syndicated column that he began
to write after he quit of 'frictions' between Ford
assistants and 'the ongoing Nixon staff under
General Alexander Haig.' Reporters learned from
terHorst in his column and after he resigned that
Mr. Ford in early September was 'spending an
inordinate amount of time soothing his own loyalists
and placating the sensitive feelings of Haig.'
There was nothing wrong, understand, with Press
Secretary terHorst's withholding knowledge that
terHorst the columnist was free to expose and
exploit. My point is simply that the numerous
reporters and commentators, including some of the
best in the business, who went practically 'ape'
over the 'open' Ford White House that they thought
terHorst bespoke and personified forgot that the
controlling function of White House press secretaries
and other official spokesmen is not to tell the
truth. It is to put the best possible appearance
upon what their principals do and say and, if
necessary in the course of that endeavor, to conceal
the truth. What my brethren in the White House

141

press room were really celebrating, during the
halcyon interlude that ended with the pardon of
Richard Nixon, was the departure of Mr. Nixon and
the quaint illusion that concealment and deception
departed with him. . . . "[10]

A concluding quotation from Nessen at the
Gonzaga symposium of 1978 gives some insight into
the impact of his wire-service and broadcasting
background on his service as Press Secretary:

"I told the President that some of my personal
traits, having a thin skin, being sensitive to
criticism, being overly sensitive to what I saw
as criticism of him, of not having the same kind
of rather relaxed, low-key, easy-going manner that
he had in dealing with the press, perhaps was
detrimental to his relationship with the press and
therefore to the public and that he might want to
think about a press secretary who had a more easy-
going personality such as his. We were on an
airplane at the time and he reached over and grabbed
my leg and said, 'Look, you're doing a fine job.
I like what you are doing, just keep doing it and
forget about the criticism.' That was the end of
the episode."[11]

---

[10]Osborne, op. cit., pp. 9-10.

[11]The Presidential Press Secretaries' Forum:
April 1, 1978, Campus of Gonzaga University, p. 2.
Elliott Roosevelt was a co-chairman of this event.

CHAPTER ELEVEN

BACKGROUND OF PRESS SECRETARIES (V)

Jody Powell has been the personable Press
Secretary for President Jimmy Carter; he has had
reasonably good rapport with the White House
correspondent corps. Although its members know
he is loyal to the President, they respect his
ability to provide authoritative information.

He gets good marks in comparison with his
immediate predecessors, although some positive
things were said about them too. Nearly every
columnist, Washington correspondent or any journalist who has regular dealings with the White House,
indicates that the most important thing necessary
in a successful Press Secretary is that he be able
to speak authoritatively for the President.

This comment by ABC correspondent Ann
Compton, now on Capitol Hill but a White House
correspondent from December 1974 to January 1979,
illustrates the point:

"Jody Powell has one great strength Ron
Nessen didn't have. He grew up in a county near
Plains, Georgia. He was with Carter ever since
1966, and he knows how Jimmy Carter thinks. When
you ask him a question, you know the answer is a
true reflection of the man he works for. Watching
his moods is often an accurate reflection, though
not always, of Jimmy Carter's moods. . . ."[1]

Jody Powell's Training and Early Background--
Although the background of Jody Powell in terms of
formal training differs from that of his recent

---

[1]Telephone interview with Ann Compton, ABC
News, November 16, 1979.

predecessors, his experience in dealing with the news media is considerable.

Powell, who was originally from the Americus, Georgia, area, had his formal training at Emory University in Atlanta as an undergraduate. He was working on a graduate degree at Georgia State University in Atlanta, as a political science major, when he joined the campaign of a relatively obscure State Senator, Jimmy Carter, to seek the Georgia governorship. Despite a loss of the governorship to Lester Maddox in 1966, Carter has had Powell on his staff most of the time since then. Powell's experience as a statehouse press secretary for Governor Carter came during the period between 1971 and 1974 in Carter's gubernatorial term. In this sense his background parallels that of James C. Hagerty, a press secretary for Governor Dewey of New York before joining the Eisenhower campaign and later going to the White House, and that of George Christian, who had served Governors Price Daniel and John B. Connally of Texas before going to work for President Johnson.

What Powell may have lacked in formal journalistic training, he perhaps compensates for with his political science background. He is knowledgeable about campaigning as well, since he served as Carter's principal press aide in the 1970 gubernatorial campaign. Powell's political science training no doubt may have been more media-oriented than it might have been earlier, since political communications and public opinion are an important part of most political scientists' programs today. But journalists' respect for him no doubt grows out of his experience in dealing with the media in two campaigns and in the Governor's office prior to the White House period.

Before arriving at the White House to serve with Carter, Powell had principal responsibility after his statehouse service in Atlanta for press

144

and media relations in the Carter presidential
campaign. This meant that he went through various
campaign crises with the then-former Governor,
including the setback in Massachusetts, the "ethnic
purity" controversy, the euphoric convention period
when Carter appeared to have a long lead over Ford,
and the debates and controversy over the _Playboy_
interview prior to November 1976. Thus Powell was
seasoned before reaching Washington. Barry Jagoda,
television adviser to President Carter for two
years, said that the media may have viewed Powell
as somewhat more partisan than a former journalist,
but this did not appear to be a major difficulty.[2]

Powell's role was significant in the presidential campaign, in which he probably had visibility
second only to that of Hamilton Jordan, the President's principal strategist. Those who have
described the Carter campaign press operation have
included Kandy Stroud, Robert Shrum (who joined
the Kennedy campaign in late 1979), and Elizabeth
Drew.[3]

Powell's background in dealing with the media,
and his considerable knowledge of politics doubtless
were a great factor in his relatively good reputation
as a Press Secretary. No Press Secretary is completely without problems, however, and some diffi-

_____

[2]See my interview with Jagoda as detailed in
William C. Spragens, _The_ _Presidency_ _and_ _the_ _Mass_
Media _in_ _the_ _Age_ _of_ _Television_ (Washington:
University Press of America, 1978), pp. 283-292.

[3]See Kandy Stroud, _How_ _Jimmy_ _Won_ (New York:
William Morrow & Co., 1977); Robert Shrum, _Running_
for _President_ (New York: Pocket Books, 1977);
Elizabeth Drew, _American_ _Journal:_ _The_ _Events_ _of_
_1976_ (New York: Random House, 1977). See also
Jules Witcover, _Marathon_ (New York: Viking
Press, 1977).

145

culties were encountered at the time of the Lance
resignation in 1977 and at the time of the 1979
Camp David "domestic summit", but these appear to
be exceptions to Powell's generally positive
record as the leading figure in the Carter White
House Press Office.

Members of Powell's Press Office Staff--The
principal deputy in the Powell office has been
Rex Granum. Some correspondents indicate that
Granum has not had a major delegation of authority
from Powell, but in the various interviews no
correspondent has denied that he has performed
satisfactorily. Granum does come from a journalistic
background, and was widely known among Washington
journalists before coming to the White House.

In the television adviser's role, Barry Jagoda
came to the White House with a background of
experience in the Carter presidential campaign.
He had also been a producer for both the National
Broadcasting Company and the Columbia Broadcasting
System prior to the 1976 campaign. He left the
White House after two years and continues to work
with his own public relations firm in Washington.

Jagoda felt it was important to keep the
President informed about various aspects of the
internal workings of major news organizations.[4]
His background made it possible for him to do this.

On Jagoda's departure from the White House,
Gerald Rafshoon served President Carter as a media
relations adviser with the title of Assistant to
the President for Communications. Rafshoon had been
the principal figure in the 1976 Carter media campaign. In that capacity he was responsible for
preparing the campaign documentary film which was
shown to the delegates at the 1976 Democratic

---

[4]See Spragens, op. cit., pp. 283-292.

National Convention in New York. Segments of this were shown as campaign "spots" (from one to five minutes) during the fall campaign of Mr. Carter in 1976.

At the time of Rafshoon's designation in 1978, he was given the task of informing the public about the operation of the President's decision-making advisers in the field of economic policy among other things.[5]

Among public relations professionals, Rafshoon was respected for his successful use of media techniques in the 1976 campaign. He moved from the White House to the Carter-Mondale 1980 Committee late in 1979. After a third-year lag in the President's effectiveness rating in public opinion surveys, common to nearly all administrations, the President's rating was rising at the time of the Iranian crisis in late 1979. It is felt that Rafshoon's work at the White House may have been a contributing factor to this, although he had left for the campaign by the time the crisis deepened in November and December of that year.

---

[5]The author's experience in Washington in 1978 included an opportunity to learn that the Rafshoon office was collaborating with political adviser Tim Kraft and the Democratic National Committee in notifying congressional candidates of the President's policy speech on inflation in October of that mid-term campaign year.

CHAPTER TWELVE

AIDES' VIEWS OF WHITE HOUSE PRESS SECRETARIES

One useful insight into the activities of White House Press Secretaries can be found in the opinions and attitudes of their fellow staff members towards them. Some of this kind of material can be found in staff memoirs. Other information can be drawn from special interview material as used in this chapter.

I have chosen to consider those aides who served with the Press Secretaries from the Kennedy Administration to the present.

Kennedy Staff's View of Salinger as Press Secretary--In commenting about the Kennedy staff's general working relationship with regard to each member of the staff, Arthur Schlesinger Jr. indicated that there was much esprit de corps among all staff members. He said this was prompted in part by President Kennedy's magnetism and charm.[1]

As for Pierre Salinger, Schlesinger noted that Salinger saw the President all the time. Kennedy was very accessible to his personal staff, according to Schlesinger, who noted that "one could get to him on the phone." Schlesinger added: "Pierre was in the office frequently and (McGeorge) Bundy (National Security Affairs adviser) also saw him several times a day. Normally there were only three in the press office to assist Salinger."

---

[1]Comments drawn from personal interview with Professor Schlesinger, July 12, 1978, at his office, Graduate Center, City University of New York.

A general statement made by Schlesinger about the Kennedy staff could be considered to include Salinger. According to Schlesinger: "In the recruitment of talent, President Kennedy picked people who were mature people. They learned to check with each other and worked relatively well together. Kennedy himself facilitated this good working relationship. Robert Kennedy had a first class mind."

Schlesinger also noted that Salinger, in addition to writing With Kennedy, has also published a book in French.[2] This book is entitled Je suis un americain (I am an American) and was published in Paris in 1975.

A close associate of Theodore Sorensen, the President's principal adviser, was Myer Feldman who was responsible for speech-writing during the Kennedy Administration along with Sorensen and others. These views of Salinger indicate his recollection of the role Salinger played in the White House.

Concerning his impressions of Salinger, Feldman commented: "Salinger had a very slow start. He began during the campaign. He was completely inexperienced, but he learned quickly. By the time we went to the White House he was an 'old pro'; he was relaxed and the President would tell him everything. He was given credit by the press corps for being honest. He was popular with the staff. If he felt they should

---

[2]Schlesinger interview, July 12, 1978. Also Kennedy staff relations are dealt with in greater detail in my paper, "John F. Kennedy and His Advisory Staff", presented at the Midwest Political Science Association annual meeting, Chicago, April 1979.

restrain themselves from something, he would[3] mention it. He was a good Press Secretary."[3]

Concerning Salinger's working relationship with the other members of the staff, Feldman's recollection was:

"He normally didn't sit in. But he did sit in at the Wednesday morning breakfast which was attended by the President, the Vice President, Salinger, myself, Dean Rusk, Ted Sorensen, and Walter Heller. We would meet for breakfast the morning before the press conference. We would make a prognosis of what would happen. He didn't attend meetings when policy and options were being discussed."

My inference from this statement is that, in order to avoid confusion, Salinger normally didn't attend such meetings. But by Salinger's own comment in a separate interview, he had input into the decisions so he didn't mind this practice.

Regarding Salinger's political skill and his human relations ability, Feldman was complimentary. He stated: "He got along with everybody very well, and was personally acceptable to everybody. His personal skills were good. He was not really a politician. He wasn't a politician in the technical sense, but he knew a lot about dealing with people so he was good in that sense."

In comparing Salinger's task as Press Secretary with that of Jody Powell, Feldman commented: "In the Kennedy years there was much more concern

---

[3]Material from personal interview with Myer Feldman, November 20, 1978, at the offices of Ginsburg, Feldman and Bress, 1700 Pennsylvania Avenue, N.W., Washington, D. C.

with national and international programs and the manner in which they were developing and operating them. (A reference to the interests of the correspondent corps.)

"Today they're much more investigative. They're looking for 'chinks'. There are more personal questions, such as what are the President's relations to Hugh Carter. They start with an investigative frame of mind. It reflects a new muckraking era in which we live. The correspondent corps helps to make public opinion and also reflects the public's interests."[4]

This tends to confirm the comment by Salinger that the task of a Press Secretary today had become much more difficult.

In writing about Salinger, Ted Sorensen refers to him as "a superb campaign press secretary" and notes that "there was an atmosphere of conviviality in the Kennedy (campaign) press entourage, encouraged by Salinger's efficient arrangements for their baggage, transportation, accommodations, instant speech transcripts and inflated crowd estimates from friendly local officials, and heightened by the attitude of enthusiasm and gaiety which spread from the candidate to his staff to the press."

Sorensen also noted: "Press Secretary Pierre Salinger's work was more closely followed by the President on a daily basis than that of any other staff member, with the exception of O'Donnell and Mrs. Lincoln. While maintaining good relations with his counterparts in both the Soviet Union and Allied nations, Pierre did not intrude on Presidential policy-making. Transcripts of his twice-daily briefings of the press were quickly read by

---

[4]Additional material from Feldman interview, November 20, 1978.

the President and staff for both illumination and
entertainment. . . . "[5]

In addition, according to Sorensen, "Salinger
and his staff and Ted Reardon checked routine
speech drafts, and my staff and Bundy's checked
major statements on domestic and foreign policy
respectively."[6]

A general comment by Sorensen: "In the White
House Pierre Salinger was superb, but Kennedy was
his own best presidential Press Secretary. His
activities, aims, announcements and family domi-
nated the news, and exclusive interviews with the
President, once a rare event in journalism, took
place almost daily."[7]

Another recollection of Sorensen's: "O'Donnell
and Salinger--and usually Bundy, O'Brien and myself--
were in and out of the oval office several times
a day. No appointment was necessary for most of
these quick informal visits, but we did not interrupt other conferences, and O'Donnell often
suggested when we might catch him between
appointments. . . . "[8]

Salinger and a military aide usually traveled
with Kennedy on his trip to Cape Cod or Palm Beach
for a working weekend. Sorensen indicates how
Salinger set up arrangements for a television
exchange between Kennedy and Khrushchev, permitting

_____

[5]Theodore C. Sorensen, <u>Kennedy</u> (New York:
Harper & Row, 1965), pp. 117, 186, 187, 264.

[6]Sorensen, <u>op. cit.</u>, p. 285.

[7]Sorensen, <u>op. cit.</u>, p. 311. See especially
Chapter XII, "The Press", pp. 310-326.

[8]Sorensen, <u>op. cit.</u>, p. 374.

Kennedy to be seen and heard in the Soviet Union, and describes some of the media relations problems Salinger dealt with at the time of the Cuban missile crisis.[9]

Various other members of the Kennedy staff, including Richard Goodwin and Richard Neustadt, were known to have a high regard for Salinger's ability as Press Secretary.

Johnson Staff's View of Reedy, Moyers and Christian--The other members of President Johnson's staff from time to time expressed their views about his various Press Secretaries--George Reedy, Bill Moyers, and George Christian.

Walt Whitman Rostow, national security affairs adviser to President Johnson after the departure of McGeorge Bundy, made these observations about the Press Secretaries:

"When I came over there in April 1966 Bill Moyers had been there for some time. I'd known Bill, got on well with him, had a lot of affection toward him. By this time his mind was on his next job. As for George Christian, he spent a lot of time in my shop before he took over. I opened up my shop to him, and we became very close friends as we are today. We went through a lot together in the latter part of that term. George Christian and Tom Johnson were at the Tuesday luncheons. But, for example, in autumn 1966 on the trip through Asia when Bill Moyers was press secretary, we worked very congenially. One reason why it worked well was that President Johnson brought his press secretaries deeply into the decision-making process. People felt comfortable raising all sorts of views. And, incidentally, contrary to a widely held impression, President Johnson was

---

[9]Sorensen, op. cit., pp. 557, 693, 697.

very knowledgeable in foreign policy. . . . "[10]

Professor Rostow described the Johnson press secretaries he dealt with as "capable", and he added: "George Christian was one of Johnson's press secretaries who ranks with Hagerty in this job. His success was built upon an extraordinary degree of credibility with the press. He wasn't lying to them and he was very sympathetic to their problems. In 1967 and 1968 the inside relations with the press (the mechanics of White House news-gathering as opposed to the outside impression given the public) were very good. George rarely spoke up at the Tuesday luncheon meetings, but he was treated as a senior adviser. Generally he just listened, but he felt free to enter in when he wanted to."[11]

Concerning his views about the ideal role of the Press Secretary, as viewed by another staff person, Rostow's views were as follows:

"It's hard to define. His first duty is to serve the President. A wise Press Secretary understands that if he is to serve the President well, he will develop a role of mutual respect with the press and also an extraordinary repu-tation for integrity. There has to be an understanding that he cannot at all times tell the press everything he knows. It should be a two-way street. We had an awful time when he (the President) went up to Canada once. The President couldn't tell the press until the last minute because it looked as if war would break

---

[10]Material based on personal interview with Dr. Walt Whitman Rostow, at the Lyndon Baines Johnson Library, Austin, Texas, August 29, 1978. See also Walt Whitman Rostow, The Diffusion of Power (New York: Random House, 1974).

[11]Rostow interview, August 29, 1978.

out in the Middle East. The President didn't
make his decision to go until after the morning
intelligence briefing. But he couldn't very
well disclose this to the press without creating
alarm. There are real conflicts between what's
comfortable for the press corps and what's necessary for a President. It's awfully hard to write
down rules here because you come back to some
very old-fashioned things like integrity. Next
to integrity, a sense of humor is an extraordinarily important part of public life. In the
Nixon tapes what struck me most was how little
sense of humor was reflected. The reason for
it is that we're frail human beings and we need
a sense of perspective. We're human beings
trying to get along. Secretary Rusk noted that
the problems we dealt with ought to be approached
on our knees. Problems ought to be approached
with a sense of humor, a sense of proportion.
George (Christian) had that quality. We had to
have it those last two years. Some truly tragic
and revolutionary things were happening. Nevertheless, we remained a group with high morale
to the end. We came through things well and the
transition (to the Nixon period) was a model job.
There was a great deal of mutual loyalty and
affection. Rusk and the President had been
together for eight years. Both Johnson and
Kennedy had a gift for making it so; in the normal course of living in a highly bureaucratic
world, you do not get to know human beings
awfully well. But it's different in looser
structures. I found that out in my life when I
started being a junior counsellor in a summer camp.
You made very close friendships. It was the same
in government. It was very important to you at
that stage because you were dealing with situations
requiring mutual dependence. You made abiding
ties with other people. Devotion to a common
purpose strengthens these associations, although
you're always conscious of a gap between responsibility (which the President has) and advice

156

(which is all you give). When you've got a
President you admire you have a sense of true
humility. I was trying to help a fellow who
had these terrible responsibilities. I've sat
in on a lot of meetings with chiefs of state,
but as soon as staffs start to get impressed with
themselves they ought to go somewhere else. I
never collected any press clippings. I got my
name in the papers but I was just working for the
President and the government, and that was
that."[12]

As for Rostow's view of the White House staff
and the White House Press Office, this was his
assessment:

"In the end the kinds of people on that staff,
the way they relate to the President and each other,
all depend on the President. They're reflections
of the kind of men he wants around him. It's
extraordinary that despite a huge bureaucracy the
style of each President and his staff eventually
seems to suffuse the bureaucracy. I was in Washington in FDR's time, in Truman's, Eisenhower's,
Kennedy's and Johnson's. There are no rules here
that are universal. When a man becomes President,
he already has developed a working style, his own
methods of organizing his business. All goes
back to the character and working style of the man
who's been elected President.

"Policy-making is more than bureaucratic
politics. The Cabinet members indeed reflect aspects of the President's multiple responsibilities,
but policy is not settled by compromise among the
bureaucracies. It is settled by the President.
You can't get inside a President's head, and that's
frustrating to political scientists and other
students of the Presidency. But policy-making

---

[12]Rostow interview, August 29, 1978.

is a much more private process of net assessment than can be imagined by a political scientist trying to find the answers just by studying the workings of the bureaucracy."[13]

Another former member of the Johnson staff, Harry Middleton, now executive director of the Lyndon Baines Johnson Library, did not comment specifically on Press Secretaries, but he did have this to say about the working relationships of the Johnson staff:

"I think the staff had a good working relationship with the President. It is now accepted as fact, but in a lot of places I've read about the Johnson White House that LBJ was an intimidator; I suppose there is some element of truth in that, but I've never known anyone who was more expert at and desirous of drawing opinions from his staff. Access was open. Opinions were invited (from the staff). There was also ready access to prepare memos for his 'night reading'. We didn't want to abuse it, but it was there. He would read it and respond."[14]

In her insightful memoirs written during President Johnson's retirement years, Doris Kearns notes that one of those with whom Johnson discussed the possibility of withdrawing from politics in late 1967 was George Christian.[15]

Nixon Staff's View of Ziegler, Warren and Klein--In the Nixon era, William Safire, a White

_____

[13]Rostow interview, August 29, 1978.

[14]Material based on personal interview with Harry J. Middleton, Executive Director, at Lyndon Baines Johnson Library, Austin, Texas, June 20, 1979.

[15]Doris Kearns, Lyndon Johnson and the American Dream, pp. 342-343.

House speechwriter, has indicated that "at the start of the administration, Nixon and Haldeman did not want a press secretary, just a low-level spokesman, or assistant in matters dealing with the media, but Ziegler fought for the traditional title and was grudgingly given it; on the first European trip, Haldeman put the Press Secretary on the bottom of the protocol list to show the low estimation of the job, but Ron quickly climbed up despite his demeaning line of work."[16]

Safire also refers to an early Nixon directive that the White House staff members should not talk with representatives of the St. Louis Post-Dispatch, the New York Times, or the Washington Post. But he added: "Fortunately, most of these strictures wore off after a while, or were eroded carefully and gradually by Klein, Ziegler, and especially (Patrick) Buchanan, who was so totally trusted to be anti-press that he could get away with fraternization. . . . "[17]

Nixon speechwriter Ray Price tells of a conference he held with Ron Ziegler in preparing a speech for President Nixon in April 1973 regarding developments in the Watergate situation.[18]

An interesting vignette indicating the working relationship within the Nixon White House is provided by Jonathan Schell, who comments:

"During the month of April (1970), several of the President's top aides began to question whether the images that the Administration was promoting

---

[16] William Safire, Before the Fall: An Inside View of the Pre-Watergate White House (New York: Belmont Tower Books, 1975), pp. 351-352.

[17] Safire, op. cit., pp. 345-346.

[18] Raymond Price, With Nixon (New York: The Viking Press, 1977), pp. 97-100.

were the best ones available. John Ehrlichman,
who now concerned himself primarily with domestic
affairs, wrote on April 15th to Haldeman, 'Among
young business executives, among municipal officials
and on the campuses we are epitomized by the Vice
President, the Attorney General, and Judge Carswell.
We are presenting a picture of illiberality, re-
pression, closed-mindedness and lack of concern for
the less fortunate. . . . I do not sense any
existing activity on the part of Herb Klein, or,
for that matter, Ron Ziegler, to respond to this
dilemma.' . . . " This brought a directive from
Haldeman to Jeb Magruder to work on a change to
promote a more positive image of the Nixon
Administration.[19]

The Nixon staff has not talked a great deal
about the working relationship, but these give
some clues to the way in which the Press Secretary
was regarded by his fellow staff members.

Ford Staff's View of terHorst, Nessen--The Ford
Administration was served by two Press Secretaries,
Jerald F. terHorst, and Ron Nessen. What did
their associates think about their White House
service?

In reflecting on other aides' views of Nessen
and the White House correspondent corps' views of
Nessen, John Osborne stated:

". . . Nessen is obsessed with the escapist
notion that his principal problem is neither
himself nor his President but the poisoned press
room atmosphere that he found in the wake of
Watergate and Ronald Ziegler. . . . There is a
fundamental, unavoidable conflict between press
secretaries and the press and Nessen frets about
it more than he should.

---

[19]Jonathan Schell, The Time of Illusion (New
York: Alfred A. Knopf, 1976), pp. 87-88.

"President Ford said of Nessen in Nessen's presence the other day, 'I think he's doing a helluva good job.' Nessen groaned in mock dismay, 'Oh God, there goes my credibility.' On the whole, though many in the press room would disagree, the facts support the President's judgment. Nine press conferences in six months, a dozen or so individual interviews, and many more background conversations, quickie chats with reporters and editors, and group sessions with television, radio and printed media news executives constitute, as Nessen says, a record of presidential access that Richard Nixon neither wanted nor tried to match. The question is what of substance comes out of it all, and the answer is very little.

"Nessen's establishment, including peripheral staffs and activities that were under President Nixon's directors of communication, has been reduced in personnel from 58 to 45. It includes two deputy press secretaries, six assistant press secretaries, two television advisers and five photographers. One of the deputy secretaries, Gerald Warren, four of the six assistant secretaries, and three of the five photographers are survivors from the Nixon time. Mrs. Ford's press secretary, Sheila Weidenfeld; her assistant, Patti Matson; and their office secretary, Nancy Cherdon, operate independently of Nessen but accept without exactly welcoming occasional guidance from him. Gerald Warren, two assistant press secretaries and three other assistants at 'professional' levels have three principal functions. They are seeing to it that department and agency officials and press spokesmen understand and accurately reflect administration policy as it is stated and amended by the President and Nessen; correcting and countering what Warren considers to be errors of fact or judgment in printed and broadcast comment; and providing print and broadcast journalists outside Washington with the nearest possible equivalent of the information, propaganda, and official briefings that journalists

161

in Washington get. Preparing the President's daily news summary, a Nixon service retained by Mr. Ford, may have been put in Warren's bailiwick when this is read. . . ."[20]

Carter Staff's View of Powell, Rafshoon--The Carter White House staff in general is understood to be highly satisfied with the performance of Press Secretary Jody Powell and Gerald Rafshoon, who served as communications adviser for a time during the Carter Administration.

My own investigation indicates that a rather high degree of esprit existed in the Carter White House. Television adviser Barry Jagoda, who served for two years in the White House, felt that despite the relatively strong loyalty of Powell to the President, he was "a more successful press secretary than anyone since Hagerty."[21]

At the end of 1979, a feeling existed among the public as well as reported views of White House aides other than Powell that the President's standing with the public had been improved by his calm, firm handling of the Iranian crisis which many felt made him look more "presidential". This is a matter for which one must assume Powell may wish to share credit with Hodding Carter III of the State Department, but it indicates his performance continues to be highly regarded in many places.

---

[20]John Osborne, White House Watch: The Ford Years (Washington: New Republic Books, 1977), pp. 86-87.

[21]See my The Presidency and the Mass Media in the Age of Television (Washington: University Press of America, 1979), pp. 283-293.

CHAPTER THIRTEEN

CORRESPONDENTS' VIEWS OF WHITE HOUSE

PRESS SECRETARIES (I)

<u>Newspaper</u> <u>Columnists</u> <u>and</u> <u>Their</u> <u>Views</u>--The
Washington correspondent corps is far from mono-
lithic. Differences abound in the character of
those who report to the public on national government and politics. But one of the most important
categories of those who do so remains that of newspaper columnists.

Several syndicated newspaper columnists are
particularly prominent. Among these are Marquis
Childs and Joseph Kraft, who write regularly about
White House matters as part of their coverage and
commentary on national and international news.

Marquis W. Childs has written for many years
for the St. Louis <u>Post</u>-<u>Dispatch</u> and for the United
Feature Syndicate. In commenting on relative
standing of press secretaries since James C. Hagerty with the Washington correspondent corps, Childs
stated that he would say the most effective press
secretary he has dealt with would be Pierre Salinger. "He was certainly the most aggressive one.
The answer depends on the closeness of the individual to the principal. Salinger had a closeness
to Kennedy. This was a considerable part of his
success. George Reedy suffered from a lack of
confidence on the part of his principal. . . ."[1]

---

[1] Personal interview with Marquis W. Childs,
October 27, 1978, <u>Post</u>-<u>Dispatch</u> Bureau, 1701 Penn-
sylvania Avenue, N.W., Washington, D.C. Earlier
I quoted from this interview about President
Johnson's relationship with George Reedy, one of
several Press Secretaries who served him.

"(George) Christian had a quieter time. Poor old Reedy was under terrible stress. That was an illustration of the importance of lack of confidence of the principal. In the Nixon era, it was largely a show that was run by people higher than the Press Secretary: Haldeman and Ehrlichman. The Press Secretary was not a very important figure. Ron Ziegler went through hell at the time when the investigative reporting was going on about Watergate and all he could do was deny and deny, Which wasn't very effective. You may remember what he said when the thing was open and shut--that everything was 'inoperative'.

"Like others, he had come out of advertising and television. I suppose he was very able in managing the TV operation. In the Ford era, the unfortunate thing at the beginning with terHorst (reference to resignation over Nixon pardon) grew out of the lack of a confidential relationship between him and his principal. There was no advance notice of the pardon of Nixon. During the (1976) campaign that proved to be a fairly difficult office. He (Ford) is a frank, honest man. After that Ford got along well with his press secretary. I always thought terHorst was a little impetuous about this and exploited it for his own interest. I suppose you can't blame him for that."[2]

Regarding style of expression, scheduling, interaction and other work habits of each Press Secretary, Childs noted:

"As to scheduling, everything depends on the degree to which you can work with your principal. If he gives you an idea of what he wants about scheduling and sticks to it, then there's no problem. If he does as Johnson did, then scheduling is a very difficult part of the work of the Press Secretary. As to style and response, a great deal depends on the political standing, or perhaps more precisely the popularity of the President himself.

_____

[2]Childs interview, October 27, 1978.

"Someone was talking with me the other day about changes in this respect, noting a more hardboiled attitude (on the part of the press).

"In Roosevelt's time, it was commonly agreed that no photograph would be taken of him in his wheelchair. It's hard to imagine that today.

"One of the things that has to be taken into consideration in this job is the fantastic increase in size of the press corps. About 1200 people are accredited now. Under FDR it couldn't have been more than 150 or 200. That enormously complicates the work of the Press Secretary."

Regarding the transformation of technology in the period from Hagerty to Powell, Childs observed:

"It's fantastic the way in which the nature of the operation has changed--it has changed by reason of the dominance of television. I think it is dominance. The power of the President to request time to address the nation or even issue public statements is tremendous. One of the problems of Johnson's Press Secretaries is that they felt the networks had been used this way far too often. That's the kind of problem this new order brings about. If you're dealing with the very powerful private enterprises that dominate the communications field, it takes a lot of stubborness, tact, or whatever to do it."

Concerning a question as to whether he found any evidence as to the degree to which each Press Secretary reflected his President's style, Childs responded:

"That's probably true of Salinger. He was a bouncy guy out there in front. He reflected Kennedy in a way. That's the only one since Hagerty of whom that's been true. Hagerty was about the smoothest press secretary I've ever seen. He had the sanction of the President. He was really able to handle it. (A reference was to the full disclosure during Eisenhower's first illness.)

You've got a lot of pushy press types over there who want to raise a flag for their particular prejudices. Comparisons like that are difficult to make, and Press Secretaries work under difficult and different circumstances.

Childs was asked whether there was a difference in types of questions according to the media correspondents work for, and he replied: "Under certain circumstances, the print people are looking for things others don't look for. Also this may be done in a more private and less open way, depending less on news conferences and briefings and more on outside investigative reporting."

The columnist was also asked whether editorial conferences and instructions from the management of dailies were a major influence on news conferences and briefings. His comment was: "Sure, that's a part of it. The editor has some idea in his head and he wants to try it out. So he suggests to the correspondent that he put it up to the President at his press conference. Another thing TV has done is the live televising of press conferences. The Press Secretary has to anticipate questions that will be asked, so there's a rehearsal of those questions beforehand and a rundown before the conference. That's a very different part of the job today.

"Truman's Press Secretary (Charlie Ross) had a particularly difficult job because while Truman's conferences were not televised live, Truman's transcript of the conference was made available after the conference. Truman made quite a few boo-boos that required correction which added to the difficulty of the Press Secretary's assignment. When Truman was on the road in 1948, when they felt it was his 'last hurrah', they (the press) treated him with contempt. They were waking Ross up at 3 or 4 o'clock in the morning. He took a beating. When a President is in a powerful position, a correspondent would like to keep access to the President as open as possible.

166

That was not true for poor Ross and Truman (when Truman was down in the polls). I felt terribly sorry for Ross, who was a good friend of mine, and I was disgusted with some of these hotshots."

Amplifying on changes growing out of the advent of radio and television, Childs commented: "There's a factor of jealousy on the part of the print media about TV, especially about TV getting so many 'breaks'."

The most significant long-term development he has seen in his Washington career, according to Childs, is "the size of the press corps and increasing competitiveness of the corps and how it impinges on the Press Secretary."

Childs felt personality traits of a Press Secretary are less important than "a real knowledge of the communications business and especially its Washington aspects. There must be a willingness to take it. Harry Truman said if you can't stand the heat you should get out of the kitchen. That can be pretty hot for a Press Secretary, even if not as much as for the man in the Oval Office. What is needed is a kind of patience."

Asked about the strengths and weaknesses of Press Secretaries, Childs commented, "I think Hagerty was the ablest and smoothest perhaps; I suppose Reedy and Nessen were two of the most deficient. I'm not at all sure that the fault was his in either case."

Concerning whether Press Secretaries see themselves as "insiders" in comparison to journalists and scholars, Childs commented: "You of course presume that a Press Secretary would be an insider; that may not always be true." He suggested the example of George Reedy, "whose usefulness was extremely curtailed by circumstances; he was probably not 'on the inside'."

As to whether the public attributes prestige for commentators in both the print media and

167

radio-TV, Childs commented:. "Prestige has a lot
to do with access. It's much easier for Brinkley
to call Jody Powell than for a correspondent with
a few papers. The head of the New York _Times_
Bureau, Hedrick Smith, could get him on the phone
whenever he wanted to. In terms of the public,
I'm not sure whether the public has any clear
impression of this matter."

Asked about competition among news media for
Executive Branch news, Childs said, "They're all
in there for what they can get. Sometimes they
get too much, I think. There are some things
that shouldn't be disclosed to anybody."

Concerning news emanating from the White
House in the pre- and post-Imperial Presidency
eras, Childs found that "perhaps there is less of
news that is genuine news, other than contrived
news or doctored news."

As to whether policy aspects or political
aspects dominate the news for a Press Secretary,
this was the view of Mr. Childs: "The policy aspects don't really figure in it very much. The
Press Secretary has to take direction from the
principal in both."

As to whether he sees himself or other
columnists carrying on in the Lippmann tradition,
Childs commented: "I don't know whether you can
put it that way. Walter Lippmann was unique.
There are those who feel they are the heirs or
inheritors of the tradition. I don't think they
are. He had a prestige and a position that I
don't think anyone has had since."

Other columnists have followed Washington
developments closely. One is reminded of Mary
McGrory, Jack Germond and Jules Witcover, James
J. Kilpatrick, Rowland Evans and Robert Novak,
Jack Anderson and others. We have presented here
the views of some of the more important significant columnists, while recognizing that there is
no unanimity among Washington columnists about

Press Secretaries and the ongoing news which the columnists seek to analyze.

Wire Service Correspondents' Views--Wire service correspondents play a unique role because their role is to distribute material to both the print and the broadcast media. Thus they serve a wide range of journalistic outlets. The Senior White House Correspondent and principal correspondent for the Associated Press is Frank Cormier; Helen Thomas holds that distinction (senior correspondent) for United Press International.

Mr. Cormier was asked what his view is of the White House setup for public information, its strengths and weaknesses. His comments were: "If you mean as it exists today, I yearn for a return to the 'good old days', when Press Secretaries were more available. (Pierre) Salinger was always available; he had an open door. You walked in and did your business. Most Press Secretaries since Salinger's time have had a closed door. (Jody) Powell won't take calls at night. He has his fingers in other pies. Maybe the White House should get someone who can devote full time to the job.

"I regret too the passing of two briefings a day. The briefing is now more in the middle of the day, although it is a kind of floating thing. Access to the Press Secretary is a big problem. His aides are not able to speak for him at least half of the time."

Concerning television news, Cormier felt he does not watch it sufficiently to make a sound answer. But he noted: "I would want to get the details in print and not on the fly. The print coverage has improved tremendously in the 17 years I have been working at the White House."[3]

---

[3]Material from telephone interview with Frank Cormier, conducted in Washington, July 15, 1979.

As to whether from a correspondent's viewpoint, a one-on-one interview or a three-on-one interview with the President is preferable, Cormier noted: "As a reporter, one-on-one is what you seek, isn't it? On a few occasions, the President has held a one-on-one interview with someone from the AP. It is more usual, however, for him to be interviewed by a small group, of four or five or eight. I like this format (small group, or one-to-one) better because there is more freedom for the follow-up questions (than in the large news conference). This is very good from our standpoint (the wire services) and his too (the President's), I hope. For example, on the flight home from Tokyo to Honolulu, we had a good opportunity for this because the AP's economics man was on Air Force One.

"In general the President's news conferences have been pretty effective. However, I was concerned with the report in the Washington <u>Post</u> today that the President is considering the possibility of abandoning the regular news conferences and feels he may use this format less and less."[4]

Cormier was queried about how Jody Powell carries off his job, and responded: "Powell can be very good really, when you can get to him. The formal briefings have almost fallen into disuse. The most productive situation is when he has a small group in his office. What I object to is that I sometimes don't know when he has one of his little seances. I miss many of those sessions. The secretaries become irritated at our hanging around outside his office.

"I strongly objected to Powell's briefings in the Middle East (at the time of President Carter's visit which resulted in the Egyptian-Israeli peace treaty).

"On the other hand, Powell conducted very

---

[4]Telephone interview with Frank Cormier, July 15, 1979.

good briefings in Vienna for the summit. At times he can be very good when he's doing those briefings. For one thing, Powell is 'plugged in' better than Salinger, for example. He can speak with greater authority. Except for perhaps Moyers and Christian during the Johnson Administration, he can't be excelled for his closeness to the President.

"As for some of the earlier Press Secretaries, no one was ever sure when Moyers was reflecting his own or the President's view of issues. Sometimes Powell's closeness to the President blinds him, as in the Lance case. There was a great deal of bitterness directed to the Washington community at the time, much of it at the press.

"Very recently he did indicate a willingness to resign from the White House staff if that would allow him to be a character witness for Lance at a federal trial; I don't take that seriously.

"As for the recent Camp David 'domestic summit', for the first few days we got virtually no information. There was no real explanation of what was going on. Then there began to be some disclosures, referred to by the press corps as the 'Sayings of Chairman Jody'. Finally he did start making conference calls to the White House press from Camp David, using a speaker phone in his office.

"As for the mass resignations of the Cabinet and senior staff (presented to Carter in July 1979), Nixon who received such mass resignations felt it was a mistake to ask for them. This occurrence, which was after the 1972 election, followed 18 days which he spent in isolation at Camp David."[5]

----

[5]Frank Cormier telephone interview, July 15, 1979. See Richard Nixon, RN: The Memoirs of Richard Nixon, Volume II (New York: Warner Books, 1978), p. 285, for Nixon's own view of this "mistake".

Mr. Cormier noted that he had worked on the White House beat since December 1962, prior to which his previous reporting experience with the AP was covering economics and finance in Washington in the Treasury press room. He commented, "One difference between that and the White House is that there were more sources there (at the Treasury and rest of economics beat). You could always, in a big agency like that, find a counter point of view on any story."

Asked about his idea of the ideal role of the White House correspondent, Cormier stated: "To be able to get at people quickly and find their responses I don't know what we can do differently than we do now, insofar as improving the correspondent's role."

He was also asked what long-term trends he sees developing in coverage, and whether technological changes will transform the media's relations to the public. His response: "Growth of television and radio have given us more money to do our work for newspapers as well. They're all our good customers. Over the past 17 years, I've seen much greater emphasis begin to be placed on the analytic piece. Once it was 'who shot John?' and now it's 'who shot John and why?' I think much more of our reporting now goes beneath the surface."[6]

Asked what presidential press conference format he prefers and why, Cormier stated: "On two occasions, Carter had about 25 reporters in for breakfast, followed by question and answer period. Breakfast was superfluous but the more conversational format that marked these sessions topped any news conference and allowed for more follow-up. I'd like to see more of this, whether or not they are called news conferences."[7]

---

[6] Frank Cormier telephone interview, July 15, 1979.

[7] Frank Cormier telephone interview, July 15, 1979.

As for preferences as to briefing format, Cormier stated, "I'm satisfied with the present briefing format, although as I noted in the interview, I'd prefer two a day."

Cormier was asked how he has seen the White House Press Office change during his time and why. He stated, "The most notable change has involved growth. Salinger had two assistants and four secretaries. Powell has six assistants in the West Wing and six secretaries. I do not believe the flow of information has increased commensurate with the staff increase."

The AP correspondent was also asked whether it would make his job easier if federal agencies' information policies were better coordinated, or whether that matters at the White House level. His comment: "I don't think this would affect White House reporters directly to any great extent."

He was asked to describe his participation in overseas coverage of the President, and replied: "Since an AP reporter is on all pools, much of my coverage when traveling, here or abroad, involves pooling, which often involves little more than body-watching. However, pooling does permit a more concentrated look at Presidents in action, and a longer look, than we normally get in Washington. Apart from pooling, overseas coverage hinges on listening to what the President and his hosts, or fellow conferees, have to say publicly, what American and other officials say at formal briefings and, whenever possible, on private contacts with U.S. and foreign officials."

As to whether he enjoys traveling to cover the President or the Vice President, wherever the trip may be, Cormier stated: "After 17 years, travel as such is only occasionally enjoyable, and most often frustrating because our chances to be tourists are limited pretty much to the view from motorcades. Professionally, it is rewarding, however, because of the more frequent and, on many occasions, more intimate glimpses we get of the President when 'on the road.'"[8]

Richard Growald of United Press International, a former White House correspondent during the Ford Administration, commented of the White House arrangement for news dissemination: "Since Hagerty's innovations under Ike, the setup has been as good as possible. The key is how cooperative the President wants to be. The writing side is good. The photo side was good only under Ford; Carter's Jody Powell is superb (in regard to) the writing press but the photo side is back in the dark days."

Regarding the quality of television coverage, Growald commented: "The quality of TV has improved, much due to technology (i. e., the more portable camera and faster processing). But it is still headline and restricted by time."

As for the format of the President's television interviews it was Growald's view that "The fewer the reporters, the easier it is for a President to slant it his way. He prefers TV because it is shallower in depth and of far wider immediate impact. He should do far more print media interviews but of course he will not."

Asked how Powell has handled the job in general, including coverage of the Lance case (1977), the Camp David Middle East summit (1978) and the energy speech and Cabinet shakeup (1979), Growald said: "Not as good as Hagerty or Salinger. Better than Nixon's Ziegler. Technically better than Nessen; but he lied on big things; (this was) not his fault but Carter's. Ford was far more honest.

Growald was on the White House beat for UPI

---

[8]The last questions were responded to in follow-up correspondence with Mr. Cormier following the telephone interview.

for three years. He commented of his work experience, "It is more glamorous than most other (beats).
But far less satisfying. It is too mechanical,
too controlled by the situation. Of course, I
now have had for three years a global and national
roving job, picking my own stories. Never the
White House again."

It was Growald's view that the ideal role of
the White House correspondent is "to tell what the
White House is doing and why and how."

Growald also responded in the affirmative
when asked whether such technological changes as
cable refinements, public access stations, television advances such as the Columbus/Houston QUBE
experiments in two-way television, mural screens,
satellites and fiber optic technology, would
change television's relationship to the public in
the coverage of political events.

As to formats for White House news conferences featuring the President, Growald said he
favors a "weekly news conference" because it provides the "best questions and most revealing
answers."

As for private briefing, Growald commented
that a "private briefing by (the) Press Secretary
is bettered only by private briefing by the President."

Concerning changes he has seen in the White
House Press Office during his time there, Growald
commented: "I served mostly during (the) Ford
period. What I have seen of Carter, Powell is
superb although lies at times like Ziegler. And
photo coverage under Powell has gone from the
openness of Ford-Kennerly to the depths of Carter-
Nixon."

Growald feels the proper role of television
in contributing to citizen knowledge and public
information is "to be the eyes and ears of the
public."

Growald took a jaundiced view of co-ordination and centralization of federal agencies' information policies. He stated, "Centralization means control. Pfui. Let 'em be disorganized. It helps getting the truth from all the paid shadow-makers."

Asked to describe his participation in overseas coverage of the President and whether he enjoys such assignments, Growald commented: "I covered Eisenhower in London, Kennedy in Germany, Johnson in Vietnam, Nixon in Moscow and Spain and Ford in Japan, U. S. S. R., Finland, Romania, Yugoslavia, Martinique, China, etc. (It's the) same as covering in D.C., with different looking background." "No (I don't enjoy it). I hate mass tour group travel."[9]

Other wire correspondents over the years have expressed varying views about White House coverage. Some of the better known ones have been Jack Bell of the Associated Press, Merriman Smith of United Press International, and Saul Pett of AP.

Wire correspondents and newspaper columnists have a distinctive view of White House reportage. Their observations can be contrasted with those of newspaper correspondents and broadcast correspondents, which will be examined in Chapter Fourteen.

---

[9]The quotations are based on a mailed questionnaire submitted to Mr. Growald and returned by him, December 31, 1979.

CORRESPONDENTS' VIEWS OF WHITE HOUSE

PRESS SECRETARIES (II)

Newspaper Correspondents' Views--White House
correspondents of major newspapers have somewhat
differing views of White House Press Secretaries
than other correspondents. Their assignments often
require more background writing, analytic probing,
and depth reporting because of the nature of their
medium.

Richard Harwood and Haynes Johnson of the
Washington Post made several references to Press
Secretaries while looking at the record of the Johnson
Administration. Harwood and Johnson commented: "On
a trip to Texas in early 1964 he spoke contemptuously
of his press secretary, George Reedy, who, he said,
'carries more useless information around in his head
than any man I ever knew. You can ask him about
oatmeal and he will talk for hours.' A few weeks
later he complained that reporters were unkind to
Reedy, 'picking at him, acting like a gladiator in an
arena . . . George knows a lot more than Pierre
(Salinger). George knows what he's talking about.
Pierre just bulled it through. He announced a lot of
things I never heard of.' . . ."[1]

Once in referring to his staff in a conversation
with the two Washington Post reporters, Johnson commented: ". . . There are three people the doctors
said they wanted to keep an eye on: Moyers, he's had
stomach trouble, and then George (Reedy), he's all
heart, can't drink and can't eat now, and then Jack
Valenti. . . ."[2]

---

[1]Richard Harwood and Haynes Johnson, Lyndon
(New York: Praeger Publishers, 1973), p. 68.

[2]Harwood and Johnson, op. cit., p. 106.

In discussing LBJ's staff changes, the two authors referred to the fact that George Reedy,"whom he once said was the man closest to him, left as press secretary and was disparaged."[3] Harwood and Johnson also mention that Reedy's departure disappointed Johnson as did the loss of Moyers, Bundy and McNamara.[4]

Concerning Bill Moyers, who succeeded Reedy in handling the media responsibilities, the _Post_ team referred to Johnson's accolade for aides who helped him with his 1965 civil rights speech: "He . . . told how wonderfully three of his closest aides had performed in helping him with that speech: 'It was mostly three men. Of course, first it was Bill Moyers. He's in on everything, he's a remarkable young man. I think he'll be dead at forty. . .'" Johnson then referred to the assistance of Horace Busby and Jack Valenti.[5]

After Moyers' departure for _Newsday_, the _Post_ reporters said: "As his problems became more serious, and as a number of key White House assistants left, Lyndon turned on them cuttingly. . . . Bill Moyers, his 'son', took the job, and then he went too, and he too was described in harsh terms. 'Moyers is not a foreign policy expert. I never had one hour's discussion of foreign policy with Moyers,' he told us in May of 1967. 'I have had ten times that amount with George Christian.' . . . Moyers could not go out to Hickory Hill and dance the Watusi and fall in the pool with the Kennedys. In Lyndon's view, Moyers was flirting with the Kennedys. That was unforgivable."[6]

---

[3]Harwood and Johnson, _op. cit._, p. 128.

[4]Harwood and Johnson, _op. cit._, p. 160.

[5]Harwood and Johnson, _op. cit._, p. 106.

[6]Harwood and Johnson, _op. cit._, p. 128.

"TRB" of the New Republic, also writing for the
Christian Science Monitor as Richard L. Strout,
refers to George Reedy's post-White House volume,
The Twilight of the Presidency, as a "splendid little
study" in which Reedy "concludes that 'some very
fundamental changes are needed in the American political system'--changes that might be adapted, he
suggests, from the parliamentary system."[7]   In
another reference to Reedy's book, Strout comments:
"George Reedy says that he originally intended to end
his book by working out 'a system of parliamentary
government for America.' He gave it up because he
decided that such a change isn't coming 'without a
revolution.' He agrees with Arthur Schlesinger on
this. But for him the failure is extraordinarily
dangerous; the system 'isolates the man who holds the
nation's highest office and shields him from reality.'
It can't last. This former adviser to Lyndon Johnson
gloomily predicts 'a man on horseback. . . . In this
probably lies the twilight of the Presidency."

In referring to then-Senator Walter F. Mondale's
book, The Accountability of Power, Strout views it
as a response to Reedy's volume, of which he says:
"The most chilling recent book about American democracy
is The Twilight of the Presidency by George Reedy,
Lyndon Johnson's former assistant, who calmly suggests
that in a generation or two we will have a Man of
Destiny in Washington keeping down crime, disciplin-
ing labor, disregarding Congress, and making the
spaceships run on time." Strout says the Mondale
book is an effort to prevent some of these things
from happening by advocating that "Congress must be
strengthened to confront the executive."[8]

While not mentioning George Christian, Bill
Moyers, or Pierre Salinger, Strout does refer to
James C. Hagerty, but only in relation to his an-
nouncements about the Soviet sputnik of 1958, the

---

[7]Richard L. Strout, TRB: Views and Perspectives
on the Presidency (New York: Macmillan, 1979), p. 427.

[8]Richard L. Strout, op. cit., p. 458.

Sherman Adams case, and the U-2 episode.[9]

The chief Washington correspondent of the
New York _Times_, Hedrick Smith, commented on the modern
White House setup for public information, its
strengths and weaknesses: "The White House news setup has strengths and weaknesses, which both flow from
the same characteristic--the Niagara of information
that is normally supplied about the President, his
family, his decisions, his activities. There is so
much information that reporters rarely have enough
time to digest it, to analyze it, to put it in perspective. Administration and White House claims
have to be reported, unexamined, because of the time-
competitive pressures.

"Of course, when the White House information on
new programs, on presidential decisions, is good and
noncontroversial, then the information flow is helpful. But often, the White House puts out a great
flood of information intended simply to monopolize
the attention of reporters, to serve as their sole
source of information. This is particularly true
during election years or other politically sensitive
periods. Quite frequently, reporters are given
texts of important speeches (State of the Union,
announcements of opening diplomatic relations with
China, grain embargo against the Soviet Union) at 6
or 7:00 p. m., with deadlines in an hour or less.
Sometimes, background and explanatory briefings are
given while reporters are being handed fairly complicated texts. The result is that no reporter has
had time to read the speech, develop his own questions
thoughtfully, and then use his access to high officials prior to publication to pursue his own questions.
Again, this gives the White House an enormous advantage in trying to put its own spin on important news
developments.

"Moreover, the tradition has developed in White
House reporting that the President's personal

---

[9]Strout, _op. cit._, pp. 177-178, 182, 200.
Similar references are made to Ron Ziegler and Jody
Powell, but Jerald F. ter Horst and Ron Nessen are
not mentioned.

movements, his church-going or his quiet family time or his jogging, is an important part of the coverage. The Presidency is covered like royalty. And this kind of coverage often drains the attention of reporters away from substantive issues, occupies their time and attention and keeps them from digging into what is actually happening behind the scenes at the White House. It is a far more complex, intricate and interesting institution than most of the content of the daily briefings would reveal.

"Another serious problem is that the pace of the information flow from the White House is so constant that very few reporters have a chance to take the White House version of events and compare it with other viewpoints.[10] Congress with its committees and its own budget office, for example, is in a position to give an alternative set of facts and figures to those put out by the White House. Not just a contrary political view, but different facts. Very few White House reporters have the time or opportunity to do that kind of comparative reporting personally. So once again, the full information policy, as it were, monopolizes the reporter. It both helps and hinders him.

"In terms of the White House news operation itself, it is hard to get a line of questioning that allows you to focus on one issue; what we get from the press operation doesn't afford much insight into the process of decision-making, such as for example, options considered and dropped, or set aside. Therefore we must look to other agencies for such information. An effort is made by some publications to do this. But this is very deeply affected by the volume of business done at the White House. Most of today's news organizations don't have the resources to do this."

In response to an inquiry about whether he felt the quality of newspaper coverage has improved,

_____

[10]Note reference to this problem in material from Bob Schieffer interview later in this chapter.

whether there's now more analysis in depth, and whether it's different working for a "newspaper of record", Mr. Smith replied: "There has been an improvement in the quality of reporting partly due to the Vietnam period and partly due to Watergate. More reporters are skeptical and less inclined to take the Administration's word for a fact. The trend over a long period of time has been toward improvement. There is a more independent frame of mind on the part of the White House correspondents. Sometimes there are excesses, with rancor or sharpness over small, niggling issues. There is today more of a sense of challenge and confrontation, and even confrontation for confrontation's own sake.

"I think there is more analysis in depth. As to recent administrations, both the Carter Administration and the Ford Administration were more open to reporters going into various agencies and getting an alternative viewpoint on things. Up to the Cabinet shakeup in July 1979 there was almost too much of this from the President's viewpoint, but not from the public's viewpoint.

"This was not true of the television networks, which are the prime source of news for most people. They are limited in terms of time, although stories such as the Iran crisis might be an exception to this.

"As for working for a 'newspaper of record', I've been with the _Times_ for 17 years so I have no real basis for comparison. It's different from the wire services; I really can't say. They don't cover the same range of issues as we do. They're often as analytic as we are but they've got a different perspective. We do concentrate on national and international coverage. I doubt that we're still a newspaper of record; those days are probably gone. The Washington _Post_ and the Los Angeles _Times_ do an excellent job on some issues, but we like to think our coverage is more comprehensive. Many people told me during the time of the _Times_ strike in 1978 that they didn't realize how much this was so until they had to depend on the _Post_ and other newspapers for coverage. Other newspapers do a good job regionally and otherwise, but we like to think that we have a balance and steadiness not found elsewhere."

Smith was asked whether recent Presidents (particularly Presidents Carter and Ford) fared better with a three-on-one format for television or print interviews. His comment: "There's no question there's a difference between the smaller groups and the large press conference. The small group can sometimes ask questions over an expanded period of time. It is seldom that a regular press conference lasts over 30 minutes; there is usually a lack of continuity. The reporters don't get a chance to explore the President's thinking carefully. Usually they come out of a press conference and have four or five different stories. This kind of fragmentation of the news is bewildering to people.

"There's absolutely a need that the President take time to meet with regional correspondents and talk about regional issues. He sat down with a group of us after the Cabinet shakeup. He talked one morning with bunch of us about the Soviet brigade issue. This is a necessary supplement."

Concerning Jody Powell's performance as Press Secretary, and his handling of recent events, such as the Lance case, Camp David summit, Cabinet shakeup and Iranian crisis, Smith commented: "I'd have a real problem making a comparison between Powell and Nessen, as I was a diplomatic correspondent during Nessen's time.

"I think Powell is basically a very effective Press Secretary for Carter. He was more effective in the first couple of years than in the third year. In late 1978 and early 1979 he became more contentious and less effective. He has basically served the President very well. He's well liked and well informed. He's rated as a steady adviser and believeable spokesman.

"The Lance case, however, wasn't handled well by the Administration, as the President put personal loyalty above his own political interests as President. Powell was affected by this personal relationship,

and was very strongly defensive. He and his operation weren't very informative about what happened
internally, even after the resignation and resolution
of the issue.

"As for Camp David and the summit with Begin
and Sadat, Jody performed particularly well. First
of all, there had been a policy decision that the
diplomacy had to be kept secret; I think he handled
this pretty well and as soon as the results were
available he was able to set it out well. Paradox-
ically, he was more available and open to the press
in the Lance case and he wound up by having the
President more damaged by this approach than at
Camp David where secrecy was imposed. Perhaps this
was because we understood the reason for the secrecy.

"As for the Iranian crisis, I can't speak to
that one terribly effectively at this time. My own
sense of it (from other reporters) is that Powell's
been pretty good. He's getting out a fairly clear
idea of what he would and wouldn't talk about."

Concerning the domestic summit of July 1979,
the President's energy speech and Cabinet shakeup,
Smith had this to say: "That was something of a
mixed bag. It was well handled after the first four
or five days. The postponement of the President's
energy speech was something of a shock; then Powell
and Jordan were in hiding for 24 hours; this served
both the President and the press very badly. On
this occasion Secretary Blumenthal had to intervene
to warn of the effect on the dollar abroad and the
gold market. There was real disarray there. However,
there's been more accessibility since then. (I can't
really say it was all handled poorly.) The blackout
at that time was probably Powell's worst period as
Press Secretary. Within a week or more he was giving
briefings at the White House and he was calling the
major newspapers. The White House was soon allowing
more visitors to Camp David to talk to the press.
It was not until the President's speech had jelled
that Jody emerged. The original speech was cancelled
around July 4 and the speech was finally given about
July 15. They were effectively functioning by July
12 or 13. The Cabinet shakeup was another difficult

184

period for 24 to 48 hours. It was amazing that
Powell wasn't present at the meeting and didn't get
a fuller version quickly. Several different versions
leaked out quickly. The press reaction and how it
would appear to the public were not taken into
account. It was the low point of the public's esteem
or approval. The effort by Powell and (Robert)
Strauss to indicate widespread negative reaction was
limited to Washington was not effective; it was a
national reaction."

Concerning his various assignments and beats
with the _Times_, Smith stated: "I've never worked
exclusively on the White House. As bureau chief I
have focused considerably on the President and on
all aspects of his Administration. I was previously
a diplomatic correspondent and a correspondent for
national security news. In that assignment I worked
at the White House, Capitol Hill, and at the State
Department. We use people that way more than other
newspapers do. Subject area specialists move in and
out of the White House, covering a field rather than
a building. This leads to more cross-rough of
official versions of government policy, and a less
simple version of the news."

As to his view of the ideal role of the White
House correspondent, Smith said, "I frankly think
that the best White House correspondent is a multiple
correspondent. One or two people have to be there,
catching flies and fielding grounders. But when they
can step back and talk to public officials in several
agencies, they are more effective. One can play the
role of chief correspondent and move around Washington
more to get a broader perspective on the Presidency."

Concerning long-term trends in coverage, print
media technological advances, and the possibility
that someday developments such as facsimile might
change newspapers' relationship to the public in the
coverage of politics, Mr. Smith commented: "I'm not
a very good seer on that. The most important change
may be when newspapers appear on a screen, or you
have a printout. But that's a long way off. In
terms of what's happened so far, the _Times_ will be
able to provide a national newspaper, not only in

185

New York but with editions for the rest of the country. As to the technical aspects, it hasn't touched us very much yet."

About his preferences regarding Presidential news conferences and Press Secretary's briefing formats, Mr. Smith observed: "As to the formats of Presidential news conferences . . . one problem is the lack of continuity which I discussed in a 1970 article in the _Atlantic Monthly_ analyzing the institution of the press conference (after Cambodia).[11]

"There's been a greater tendency by Presidents Carter and Ford both, to allow individual reporters to follow up every question. I'd favor a system of drawing by lot to get more continuity, or there might be ways of holding press conferences limited to foreign policy, e. g. But I don't think the process is going to be basically reformed.

"As for briefings, I'd prefer having those at an earlier time of day, not so late in the day. Powell is not the best organized Press Secretary we've had, but he's reliable. An earlier time would allow better followup of important news developments.

"I don't know whether you can control the cacophony.[12]

Mr. Smith independently suggested that it would be worthwhile to explore the relationship between the Press Secretary and the Press in the early period of a specific Presidency. He suggested that "a fair number of reporters are there who were covering the new President during the campaign. They have won their spurs, received a White House assignment.

---

[11]See Hedrick Smith, "Viewpoint: When the President Meets the Press", _Atlantic Monthly_, August 1970 (226: 2), pp. 65-67.

[12]For Powell's own comments on a brief period of fewer briefings and more informal meetings with correspondents in his own office, see "Speaking for Himself", _Washington Journalism Review_, May 1980 (2: 3), p. 43.

They have a stake in that the politician as a candidate and the Press Secretary from his side has a friendlier feeling toward those who went through the campaign with him and his candidate. They come to Washington and a new stream of reporters flowed into an old stream of reporters, making mixed streams there. The Press Secretary at this point doesn't get along as well with some as with others. Later on you get a certain form of disenchantment about whether the Administration keeps its promises.

"The Carter Administration has been open, and is a good example of this. You didn't see what kind of political problems would be in the new environment."[13]

Views of Broadcast Correspondents--Broadcast correspondents who were interviewed in various fashions included Bob Schieffer and Robert Pierpoint of CBS; Ann Compton of ABC, and Tom Brokaw and Judy Woodruff of NBC. The following represents an account of their views of the White House Press Office.

Concerning the strengths and weaknesses of the modern White House setup for public information, Schieffer commented: "It is very similar to the setups in all government agencies now. This has become institutionalized over the years. From the reporter's standpoint, it's as effective as any other press office as it were. From the standpoint of the press, you get handouts, that sort of thing. It's worked out over the years. The weaknesses grow out of the fact that you have so many reporters covering the White House today; you can have an access problem. Being herded on press trips, having 'pool' arrangements (shared reportage) and the like. As for covering the President himself, you're so inundated with spot news, you can't do investigative reporting. Television is the primary source of news for most people. Every appearance of the President that we

---

[13]Telephone interview with Hedrick Smith, chief of the New York Times Washington Bureau, Tuesday, December 11, 1979, and subsequent correspondence.

cover, someone has to be there just for insurance, to be sure he doesn't do the unexpected. There are a number of stories which have never made our air. He (the President) can say something of significance at the most insignificant event. He told a group of eighth graders during the campaign about his views on the B-1 bomber, for example. The kids had asked about the B-1 bomber. Being a White House correspondent is a basic kind of journalism. It's almost like the political beat or writing obits. Most of it is the five 'W's'. The title of correspondent doesn't mean one can put the news in context."[14]

To Robert Pierpoint, veteran CBS White House correspondent, the system appeared this way: "I would say it's a little hard to give you a rundown on what works the best. Speaking in general, it's pretty good. The strength of the present system is the access of the press secretary to the President himself and the ability of the press secretary to speak for the President. The weakness of the present system is the tremendous volume of work that grows out of the queries to the White House Press Office. They (the Press Office staff) want to deal with the media out in the country as well as with us in the White House press corps. In trying to go around us, they spend a great deal of time answering inquiries from all around the country; they're not really equipped for this in terms of budget and manpower. Despite this, by and large over the years, it's been pretty good."[15]

To Ann Compton, who served approximately three years on the White House beat for ABC, the matter had to be looked at in context. "You've hit a broad area with that question. Of course there are two

---

[14]Material from personal interview with Bob Schieffer, CBS News White House correspondent, at the White House, December 18, 1978. Mr. Schieffer is now anchor for the CBS "Morning" program.

[15]Material from telephone interview with Robert Pierpoint, CBS White House correspondent, August 6, 1979.

aspects of this in the White House. As for the
Office of Media Liaison, I had no dealings at all
with that; they sent out kits to local news directors
and were lavishing attention to the local media. As
for the White House system for correspondents in
Washington, it has not changed much. The system
shapes the people who work there more than they shape
the system. The White House is no more open under
Jody Powell than it was under Ron Nessen.

"The White House press corps can make the White
House news operation useful for coverage as much as
it wants to. So you can go beyond the daily briefing.
The problem is that if you have a very active President, the danger for reporters is that you get caught
up in covering mere activity more than you need to.
I was there from nearly the beginning of the Ford era
up to January 1979. It was mostly an active time,
although recently Carter hasn't been as active; both
he and Ford were quite active during much of my time
there. The biggest frustration was (to be obliged)
to cover this 'little stuff', routine events such as
the March of Dimes poster child. I found myself
struggling to get a broader perspective when I was
covering the White House during these periods of in-
tensive presidential activity."[16]

Tom Brokaw of NBC, former White House correspondent, had these general comments on the White
House structure for dissemination of news, its
strengths and weaknesses: "I think on balance it
works quite well. In this current Administration,
Jody Powell is an asset to both the President and the
reporters because he knows the President's mind and
his policies as well.

"I gather that after organizational difficulties,
the Carter White House Press Office has solved that,
and the paper flow is more efficient now.

_____

[16]Material from telephone interview with Ann
Compton, Capitol Hill correspondent and former White
House correspondent for ABC, November 16, 1979.

"From my point of view a weakness of the White House Press Office in this Administration as well as the previous Administration is that they too often think of television as a kind of personal forum rather than a medium of the press.

"One example is that they're always incensed when occasionally the networks elect not to televise a Presidential press conference.

"Also, I personally have felt strongly that television video cameras should be permitted to roll during the day-to-day press briefings."[17]

White House Correspondent Judy Woodruff of NBC observed: "Strengths would have to include the fact that information can be disseminated in a speedy, timely fashion, if it is important enough, because so many news outlets have access to the White House Press Office. Certainly, the fact that technology has transformed the news industry, both print and electronic, into the business of instant communications, well serves the public. However, the public is not well served by a White House that dominates news dissemination in Washington, and by news media which permit that domination to continue, or at least, do not actively challenge it. An efficiently run White House news operation is considered one that controls the flow of the news from the entire administration . . . in that the President's desires and policies are reflected by statements, wherever they are made. But it would be far healthier, from a public information point of view, if there were less concentration on what the President says and does, and more on the operation of the entire bureaucracy, of the entire government, as it acts, and reacts, with the citizens it serves."[18]

---

[17]Material from telephone interviews with Tom Brokaw of NBC News, December 10, 1979, and February 13, 1980.

[18]From correspondence with Judy Woodruff, NBC News, May 23, 1980.

In response to a question as to whether the correspondent corps felt the quality of coverage has improved, or whether it is still largely a headline service, these comments were made:

Schieffer: "Yes, it has improved. For instance, electronic cameras have made it possible to move forward the deadline. This has been extended four hours (closer to air time) with the new equipment. Part of our responsibility is to provide a headline service; there's nothing wrong with that. Part of our job is when we're doing a better job. We can do things more quickly. For instance, when we would fly to Vail at 11 a. m. with President Ford there might not have been time to get a good pickup for the Evening News. With the new equipment we can do that."[19]

Pierpoint: "I think it's improved because technologically it's improved. However, it's still somewhat spotty; this depends in part on the individuals involved. It's become more show-business oriented in the past ten years. There's more emphasis on a pretty face, less on experience. I would say that the general quality of television news has improved. We now have producers of pretty high quality. You have a balance in terms of the final product on the air. Because of the technological improvements, the coverage can be more up to the minute. In a serious organization like CBS News, the quality is pretty high; the quality of the (newsgathering) organization itself can be an important factor. The networks today are spending more time and money (for good news coverage) and therefore are doing a better job. But it's not all that different from television and radio coverage of 25 years ago. We do have some programs where we can do more. The CBS Morning News and Sunday Morning News are examples of this. But as you know, we're still trying to get more time for the Evening News; we need an hour rather than a half hour for that. We do have the manpower, the talent and

---

[19]Personal interview with Bob Schieffer, December 18, 1978.

the ability (for going to an hour format), but as long as we continue the present format, the coverage will continue to be two or three paragraphs of a front-page story (because of time limitations)."[20]

Ms. Compton: "Yes to both parts of your question. Television coverage has become more sophisticated and insightful. But it's still a headline service. In the old days under Nixon, White House correspondents would be covered by cameras while standing on the White House North Lawn, spending a minute and a half telling what the White House did that day. Now you will see the anchorman or the correspondent saying this is what the White House did, but there will be modern graphics in the background, or it will be followed up by a correspondent in Chicago or someone who has been to Galesburg, Illinois, to get the (grassroots) reaction there. The new technology has enhanced the White House coverage in the last five years. The cameras and studio technical advances have made much of this possible--the new electronic toys we have to play with."[21]

Brokaw: "I think it has improved, but at the same time the nature of the institution of TV--principally the limited amount of time we have--makes us, if not a headline service, mostly a kind of diary of what has happened. It's hard for us to be a medium of record. I just think that it's constantly more sophisticated as we go ahead. I think the majority of the reporting is better too."[22]

Ms. Woodruff: "Yes, the quality has definitely improved. There are more in-depth pieces done on NBC, in the form of special segments, than there

---

[20]Telephone interview with Robert Pierpoint, August 6, 1979.

[21]Telephone interview with Ann Compton, November 16, 1979.

[22]Telephone interviews with Tom Brokaw, December 10, 1979, and February 13, 1980.

have ever been done in the past. All three major
networks show flexibility, when the story warrants,
for longer, more comprehensive reports, than ever
before. There is a sense that the public wants this
kind of coverage, when it is warranted. All three
networks are putting emphasis once again on news
specials . . . and on live news coverage of major
events. There is more news on the air now, than
ever before, and new news programming is being planned
for mid-morning, and late at night, on NBC, even
now. As the networks, especially ABC, in contrast
to its historic lack of emphasis on news, realize
that excellence in news coverage helps build their
reputations, more than any other kind of programming,
the public will benefit."[23]

Correspondents were next asked whether they
thought the President should follow the three-on-
one format for television interviews, or whether he
does better with the one-on-one format as used by
Bill Moyers and James R. (Scotty) Reston of the New
York _Times_. Their responses are as follows:

Schieffer: "The President's not guaranteeing
anything (to the media); he's making news for himself.
FDR met the correspondent corps twice a week at his
desk. In campaigns, he wasn't always available but
he could be interviewed in the afternoon. All of
those things can be very effective for the President.
The number of reporters present is less important
than what the President has to say. He has to guard
against boring the public. Ford made himself so
readily available that he didn't always have that
much to say."[24]

Pierpoint: "I wouldn't want to look at this
question from the President's standpoint. From our
viewpoint (that of White House correspondents) I

[23]Correspondence with Judy Woodruff, May 23,
1980.

[24]Personal interview with Bob Schieffer, December 28, 1978.

would favor 'the three-on-one. This format allows
the questioners to give thought to follow-up questions, and it allows them to get more information
from the President. It doesn't allow the President
time to filibuster. The one-on-one format gets a
little too chummy. I think within limits it's better to have more questioners; I would however prefer
the three-on-one format to the regular press conference."[25]

Ms. Compton: "Both have advantages and dis-
advantages from the viewpoint of a correspondent.
Every form of presidential contact with the media
would have some pitfalls. With the one-on-one format, the problem is that only one mind is doing the
questioning. On the other hand with just one correspondent an articulate, aggressive reporter can
sometimes put the President to the wall. The problem
with one-on-three is that one correspondent shouldn't
try to 'hog' the time. Sometimes too, a group of
three can come off sounding too nice to the President.
They must be firm and resolute with the President,
as they can't let him get off with half-answers at
which most Presidents have proven to be masters.

"The news conference has its share of problems
too. Every President benefits by using a variety of
media techniques."[26]

Brokaw: "I've participated in both. I guess I
think Ford was better in an intimate environment
(one-on-one, two-on-one) rather than a press conference. Carter seems to be at ease, and does well,
whatever the format."[27]

_____

[25]Telephone interview with Robert Pierpoint,
August 6, 1979.

[26]Telephone interview with Ann Compton, November 16, 1979.

[27]Telephone interviews with Tom Brokaw, December 10, 1979, and February 13, 1980.

Ms. Woodruff: "I think it depends on the situation. I think there is a relationship that can be established in a one-on-one interview that cannot be duplicated when there is more than one questioner. As long as my network gets its share of those one-on-one interviews, I think they're fine. But there are times when having a group of questioners may elicit the best results . . . whether it's three or however many, those sometimes have their place. Unfortunately, I think there is a tendency in those situations, for the questioners to compete among themselves for the 'cleverest' question . . . but perhaps that's not entirely unhealthy."[28]

Correspondents were asked how they feel Jody Powell is performing as Press Secretary. They were asked specifically to comment if they wished on the handling of the Lance case (1977), the summit at Camp David with Begin and Sadat and the China recognition speech (1978), and the "domestic summit", energy speech, and Cabinet shakeup (1979).

Schieffer: "Generally, he has been a very good press secretary. His strength is that he is a policy-maker and he is truly an adviser to the President. Ron Nessen was more of a traditional type press spokesman. Having access to Jody means that reporters have access to a policy-maker in government; Jody's not the best at returning calls, though.

"As for the Lance affair, that was very poorly handled. They let their emotions take over rather than let it fall into its own perspective. But this was _very_ _difficult_ _for_ _them_. After all, Lance was perhaps the President's only close friend of his own age. As for the announcement about Chinese recognition (made in an evening speech in prime time by the President on Friday, December 15, 1978) there was a leak in the State Department before the story broke. The Administration arranged meetings before the

---

[28]Correspondence with Judy Woodruff, May 23, 1980.

speech with the network anchor men; the next day there were (background) briefings at the State Department. That's where the leak occurred (and not at the White House).

"As for spokesmen I've worked with, Jody's probably the best. Jerry Friedheim at the Pentagon (Schieffer's pre-Ford beat) under Mel Friedman was good too. They've had their successes and failures. As for the recognition of China, this shows that the White House can turn on their PR apparatus when they want to. This shows what they can do when they want maximum exposure, and generally speaking a very favorable impression was made with the media and the public."[29]

Pierpoint: "Jody Powell is probably one of the best press secretaries I've worked with in terms of being a voice for the President. Jody Powell speaks for the President and therefore he is very useful to the President. I can remember a number of press secretaries going all the way back to Jim Hagerty, who was probably the best of them all.

"I think Powell didn't handle the Bert Lance case very well because the President didn't handle it very well. I'm inclined to blame him (President Carter) rather than his press secretary. It's good to remember that the press secretary serves at the pleasure of the President. They were a group of Georgians who were new on the job. They were wounded personally (by the Lance affair) and because running a state was different from running the country, on this matter they were not up to the job. But that reflects Jimmy Carter and not his press secretary.

"On the Middle East situation, I think Jody handled it very well. He tried to avoid misleading us while allowing the President enough flexibility to achieve a dramatic effect (when the treaty was announced). He handled it pretty well.

---

[29]Personal interview with Schieffer, December 18, 1978.

"As for the 'domestic summit' and the Cabinet shakeup, that was not a good situation for Jody because it was not good for the President. He has let bitterness toward the press corps reflect itself too much; it's partly reminiscent of the Nixon Era. When the President cancelled his first speech on July 5 (on energy policy), Jody should have told him to give a reason for that cancellation. They had to come up with an explanation and the President had to be saved from himself. They went 48 hours without telling anybody anything; this shook the confidence of the media and the public in the Administration. That was dumb. It hurt the President and the Presidency. I suspect that both Carter and Powell might agree with this today. But they were just back from Tokyo (site of the economic summit); they were tired and they were hurt by the polls. There are times when a press secretary needs to persuade the President to do things differently. I'm afraid Jody Powell is emotionally not able to do that. One of the things that Jim Hagerty could do that Powell cannot do was to say, 'Mr. President, you're wrong!'"[30]

Ms. Compton: "Let me start by saying that when Ron Nessen left the White House, I was convinced that no man could possibly do well in the job. First of all, he has to serve two masters--the President and the White House press corps.

"Jody Powell has one strength Ron Nessen didn't have. He grew up in a county near Plains, Georgia. He was with Carter ever since 1966, and he knows how Jimmy Carter thinks. When you ask him a question, you know the answer is a true reflection of the man he works for. Watching his moods is often an accurate reflection, though not always, of Jimmy Carter's moods. Of course, as with most press secretaries, you eventually get the 'circle the wagons' mentality. Press secretaries get to thinking the press corps is unfair and unreasonable with their boss,

---

[30]Telephone interview with Pierpoint, August 6, 1979.

that they're 'out to get us'. About the time of the
Bert Lance affair, Powell began to slip. He diminished his ability and this has made him less easy
to deal with. I don't know of any person who can
really master the job."[31]

Brokaw: "I think that Ron Nessen was not a very
successful Press Secretary, both from a reporter's
point of view and from the Administration's point of
view. From the reporter's point of view, he often
was easily officious, high-handed, and I know for a
fact from the Administration's point of view that a
number of high level officials complained that he
wasn't able efficiently or even effectively to por-
tray their positions. I'm told on reliable authority that he was especially bad at dealing with diplomatic nuance and subtlety.

"As for Jody Powell, with the exception of
social aspects (e. g., a controversy about how he
treated reporters during President Carter's Middle
Eastern shuttle (of 1979), where he might have misled them), he's done pretty well. And he overreacted
to a story that Hamilton Jordan spit a drink down a
woman's dress. Otherwise, he has pretty good marks.

"(A) I think in terms of the Lance case there
was overreaction of both the White House and the
press which saw it as a kind of personal vendetta.
It was not the most heroic thing when Jody tried to
spread charges damaging to Senator Percy (which
proved unfounded), and I think he learned a valuable
lesson there.

"(B) (As for the Camp David Summit) "That worked
very well from their point of view. The press was
frustrated, but there is nothing in the Constitution
that says the press has to have access. Diplomacy
can be conducted in secrecy, it turns out, and can
be effective. On the other hand, we in the media
have an obligation to our readers and viewers to report as much as we can. We need to know about pledges

---

[31]Telephone interview with Ms. Compton, November 16, 1979.

and promises that might have been made, such as the West Bank. This was handled reasonably well. We found out as much as they wanted us to find out. This may sound like heresy coming from me, but sometimes the people im my profession turn over rocks just for the sake of turning over rocks. But we must get all access possible.

(C) (On the Cabinet shakeup) "This was handled abysmally because the press, other political figures and the public had not been prepared for the news. It gave the impression of being very precipitous. It was the nadir of the Carter Presidency in terms of the image he was trying to convey to the country. As for the Camp David 'domestic summit', I had great reservations about the calling of journalists to Camp David. There is something slightly askew about them sitting down with a President. This is more the function of executives."[32]

(D) (On Iran and Afghanistan) "The recent international crises they've handled very well. The press representatives of the President (Jody Powell and Hodding Carter III) have done well. However, the press should have had more access to the President."[33]

Ms. Woodruff: "I think Jody does a superb job of being a partisan spokesman for the President, although I wish he would be a little less defensive in his support. I would rather have a press secretary on the 'inside', than to have to deal with one who didn't know what was going on, even at the risk of losing some accessibility. . . . The Lance case was handled poorly because the White House was not yet accustomed to dealing with the Washington media, and they felt so close to Lance, it took them a long time, longer than it should have . . . to understand how serious the problem was that they had on their

---

[32]The implication is that the role of media people, particularly reporters and correspondents, is not to be advising the President.

[33]Brokaw interviews, December 10, 1979, and February 13, 1980.

hands. The Camp David summit was handled well, in
the sense that the press was not guided to have high
expectations of what would result, and therefore in-
terpreted it as a great victory for Carter. The domestic summit was a rather silly attempt to salvage
a very unpopular President in the midst of the gas
shortage . . . the energy speech came across as one
of the best the President's delivered with the exception of the presumption made that the American
people were suffering from some kind of 'malaise'.
Otherwise, the speech held up well. It was all dis-
sipated by the Cabinet shakeup, at Jerry Rafshoon's
suggestion . . . which made Mr. Carter look as inept
as he had originally . . . in the eyes of the Washington news media . . . and was more tolerantly received by the public at large. Even so, I think the
public saw through it as an attempt to do something
dramatic, to take attention off his other problems.
Whether it did any lasting harm, is debatable.

"As for the handling of the Iran crisis . . . I
think they milked it for publicity in a skillful
fashion for the first several months . . . using the
now-famous Rose Garden strategy. But I think once
the strategy began to backfire . . . after the failed
rescue mission . . . the President began to play
down the Iranian issue. He was most skillful at in-
timidating other presidential candidates into not
criticizing Administration policy. . . to the extent
that when Kennedy tried, the President accused him
of 'damaging the country.' . . . and the public evi-
dently bought it. If there had been another, more
electable opponent running against Carter, the President might not have gotten away with his tactic as
well as he did.

"I think finally the White House has done a
superb job of turning the Afghan invasion into a
political plus: they have made it an occasion to
rally support for an Olympics boycott . . .
rallying public opinion against the Russians, in a
way that never hurts in an election year. Whether
their tactics will help them in the long run . . .
remains to be seen. But in the short run,
Mr. Carter has certainly helped himself with the

voters."[34]

Each of the correspondents was asked how long he or she had been on the present assignment, how long they spent on the White House beat if trans-ferred and when. They were also asked to compare the White House beat with others they have experienced in their coverage.

Schieffer: "I've been here about four and a half years, since the Ford Era began. It's been en-joyable in some ways to travel. There's something special about the White House; it has its own mys-tique. In the agencies (such as at the Pentagon) you see arguments going on before recommendations are made. That's one difference. Of course, from a news person's point of view, the White House is a wonderful place to get exposure."[35]

Pierpoint: "I've been covering the White House beat for almost 23 years. I was a foreign correspon-dent, but I've found the White House beat a lot tough-er to cover. It's more exciting and it's certainly in the middle of things. It's a fascinating beat because of that."[36]

Ms. Compton: "I'm now on Capitol Hill, covering the Senate and some candidate activity; I've been there since January 1979 when I moved from the White House to Capitol Hill. I joined ABC's White House coverage in December 1974 and covered Ford's entire administration from that time up to the day he lost in November 1976. The next day after the election I flew to Plains and covered Jimmy Carter during the transition period and the first three years of his Presidency. My greatest frustration in covering the

---

[34]Woodruff correspondence, May 23, 1980.

[35]Personal interview with Schieffer, December 18, 1978.

[36]Telephone interview with Pierpoint, August 6, 1979.

201

White House is that it was a kind of 'death watch' in a way; our network has a policy to run the cameras whenever the President's plane takes off or lands, just in case. Even when Ford went to play golf in suburban Washington, the network cameras were there. I was in Sacramento with Ford September 7 (1975, the day of the Squeaky Fromme attempt on his life) and in San Francisco on September 25 (the day of the Sara Jane Moore attempt on Ford's life). When Jerry Ford, late on a week night in Hartford, Connecticut, was riding in the presidential limousine, I was riding in a travel pool with him in a station wagon, when Jimmy Salomida's 1976 model car slammed into Ford's car. You never know.

"The public has little idea of the precautions we take not to miss a major presidential news event. The network pool videotape operation is always there. The public has no idea of how many precautions and contingency plans we have--should the President say anything (important) or should anything happen to him."[37]

Brokaw: "Before the White House, I was an NBC California correspondent and was based in the West; after that I went to the White House. Before California, I was in the South covering civil rights; this was the period when Jimmy Carter was a state senator in Georgia. Where I am now, I have a broad range of concerns. But a White House correspondent has a single focus which is the Presidency. Here the whole world is my oyster. The difference is something like that between being a reporter and being an editor. The term White House correspondent conjures up a glamorous image. I was there the last year of Nixon and the first two years of Gerald Ford. It can be a little seductive. One can become used to that red carpet environment, having the story present itself to you. I'm glad I did it for that period, but I enjoy my present job now."[38]

---

[37]Telephone interview with Ms. Compton, November 16, 1979.

[38]Telephone interview with Brokaw, December 10, 1979.

Ms. Woodruff: "I have covered the White House since the day Carter was inaugurated. I prefer it to the other assignment I had with NBC (other than covering the presidential campaigns in 1976, which I loved) . . . because I grew tired of 'living out of a suitcase', as I travelled around a ten-state area, covering whatever story popped up on a given day, I like 'beat' reporting . . . I find it rewarding . . . and I am able to use my contacts with the Carter Administration, built up over ten years of covering him and his long-time aides."[39]

Each respondent was asked to consider his or her idea of the ideal role of a White House correspondent. Their comments:

Schieffer: "I suppose if we think in terms of results, the most important thing you can do is to develop sources so you don't have just an office where you receive handouts. The President is the ultimate of sources. I suppose the ideal thing would be to be able to get him on the line whenever you wanted to do so. At the level of the Presidency you sometimes get to know a President well enough (work habits, etc.) to anticipate what will happen."[40]

Pierpoint: "I think probably the ideal role is the one John Osborne is where you write every couple of weeks; you have time to think and to talk to people. With the networks, there is too much daily routine; they don't fully utilize the background of the network correspondents. There's a lot of TV and radio news time to fill. It's kind of like a wire services job and that's not ideal. It would be much better to be able to sit back and take a hard look at things. We seem to work in fits and starts, usually fits. I get calls at least once a day asking for a minute or a minute 15 (seconds) and they just

---

[39] Correspondence with Ms. Woodruff, May 23, 1980.

[40] Personal interview with Schieffer, December 18, 1978.

203

say 'Please do a broadcast' knowing there's always
something going on at the White House. This kind of
mindless thing goes on constantly because of the
system. That's why John Osborne does a marvelous
job; he has plenty of time to put things into perspective."[41]

Ms. Compton: "One thing I would ask more than
anything else would be if we did not have to rush to
a 6 p. m. deadline at night. The President nowadays
has a news conference at 4 p. m. and it's over at
4:35, which means you have an hour and 25 minutes at
most I have to be ready (for the air). I have to be
able to make a report complete. It's an impossibil-
ity. We also have a radio deadline every 12 minutes.
I think the ideal situation would be to be able to
concentrate on one story a day, or one issue a day.
If I ever went to the White House, I'd like to have
another ABC staff person there doing the regular
coverage so I could really dig into one story at a
time."[42]

Brokaw: "It would be that of the person who
gives us the best perspective on the Presidency, the
evolution of the persons there, and being able to
reach whoever it is the President has day-to-day
dealings with.

"One danger of being a White House correspondent
is that the White House correspondents group is so
close and confined in an emotional way that there is
a danger of groupthink (perhaps this is more true in
television than in anything else). You have to be
careful that your personal relationship with even
the Presidents and other White House reporters and
the White House staff doesn't become too close.
Distance is important. Also there is a tendency
while there to think of the White House as the only

---

[41]Telephone interview with Pierpoint, August 6,
1979.

[42]Telephone interview with Ms. Compton, November 16, 1979.

place in the world where everything is going on."[43]

Ms. Woodruff: "The White House correspondent should be the chief interpreter of Presidential policy and politics . . . not a specialist necessarily, on any issue, but a reporter who has cultivated extensive contacts within the White House, and elsewhere, in the Administration, on Capitol Hill, and in the opposition party. The White House correspondent cannot be expected to be an expert on any particular issue, except the personal story of the President himself, and his family . . . and the politics of the President and his advisers. This person should be fair, as every other journalist, in covering his or her beat . . . but must be constantly on guard that he or she is not swept up in the White house propaganda, too afraid to write or deliver a tough, fair story, for fear of losing access. The fear of losing access must never be a consideration for a serious journalist."[44]

Each correspondent was asked about long-term trends he or she saw developing in coverage.

Schieffer: "I really don't know. If present trends continue, you'll see more and more of persons assigned to cover a beat. This will make it difficult to cover the President and the White House. The whole business makes me very nervous. Another thing is that with the enormous audience television has, you run the risk of networks becoming lost in the shuffle, and unable to follow up on investigative reporting. I hope the other news media won't give up on this. One of the things we'd be worried and concerned about would be if the agencies were to become just official conduits for news. That problem and the screen personality problem are important ones. Look at how Barbara Walters and Walter Cronkite became in effect participants in the diplo-

---

[43]Telephone interviews with Brokaw, December 10, 1979, and February 13, 1980.

[44]Correspondence with Ms. Woodruff, May 23, 1980.

matic process, merely in the process of trying to get a story."[45]

Pierpoint: "I could only give an educated guess. I'm a reporter and I'm not paid to go into future developments like that. An executive of the network or a bureau chief would be a more appropriate person to ask bout that. I do think cable television will give us more to do. It will probably open up the possibility of such things as an all-news television station. That's good in a way, but it all depends on whether the network gives us more resources to work with."[46]

Ms. Compton: "Most of these changes will not have a major impact on White House coverage. The White House correspondent's job is a specialized function in any news organization. There will be more impact from our ability to report live from anywhere in the world. The equipment used right around the President to convey his news and actions would make the greatest difference."[47]

Brokaw: "I do worry that it might have the opposite kind of effect than the improvements I have just been talking about (in ideal coverage). Instead of bringing more thoughtful coverage, it might just bring more instantaneous reporting. We need more perspective about the evolution and development of those in the White House. That worries me about it. The cable business could be the means of Presidents circumbenting the networks. I don't know what kinds of controls cable would have, that would be the equivalent of editors, producers and so forth that

---

[45]Personal interview with Schieffer, December 18, 1978.

[46]Telephone interview with Pierpoint, August 6, 1979. Ted Turner of Atlanta began in June 1980 a 24-hour Cable News Network with the assistance of Daniel Schorr.

[47]Telephone interview with Ms. Compton, November 26, 1979.

one finds in the networks.

"What I worry about is that this could circumvent the process of the adversarial relationship."[48]

Ms. Woodruff: "I mentioned this, tangentially, in the first answer. I think, for the most part, the results are good for the public. To the extent all these modern developments and refinements, expand and increasingly emphasize, news coverage, they are healthy. To the extent, however, (that) they give politicians an added excuse to 'manipulate' the media, they are worrisome. I suppose it is inevitable that politicians will master the QUBE . . . as they have the 5 p. m. announcement for the 6:30 network news program.

"Satellites are making it possible for candidates to make an appearance as late in the day as they want . . . and be almost assured that it will make the evening news. The greater capacity for instant coverage unfortunately tempts the broadcast media to carry live those statements and actions by a President that they might not otherwise pay much attention to. The capability to 'go live' with any announcement from the White House lawn, gives the President an enormous advantage, that the news media should strive to hold in check."[49]

Three of the correspondents discussed what presidential news conference format they prefer and why.

Pierpoint: "I really think the format which has worked best is the one in which correspondents draw lots in advance for the opportunity to ask questions, and take turns at the microphones. Ford and Nessen did this and it worked very well. It does away with the possibility of the President picking 'soft touches' to ask the questions. I think it works pretty well. Another format that I like is the informal session in the Oval Office (not televised) which is

---

[48]Telephone interviews with Brokaw, December 10, 1979, and February 13, 1980.

[49]Correspondence with Ms. Woodruff, May 23, 1980.

sometimes quite effective."[50]

Ms. Compton: "There are two that I prefer and I think you have to use them together. I'd be the first to agree with my print brethren that the presence of cameras, microphones and lights changes the whole atmosphere of a news conference. But the President should be subjected to this very public kind of questioning. Just as valuable, however, is the 'quiet hour' spent with the President by a handful of correspondents, invited into the Oval Office on the spur of the moment."[51]

Ms. Woodruff: "I like the live, spontaneous format, because I think the public has a right . . . or, is well served, . . . when it can view the President handling himself in an impromptu situation. Most of the questions are anticipated, and very poorly answered, but occasionally, he will be surprised, and it is worthwhile to the public, to have this glimpse, however brief, of how his mind works.

"I would prefer also to see many more, background sessions with the President. . . . But Mr. Carter is not comfortable with the press, and I expect to see no more of them in the future."[52]

Pierpoint: "If we had briefings twice a day, at 10:30 or 11 and again at 4 in the afternoon, I'd prefer that to the present system of one briefing a day. I also think it should be put on the record and made available for radio and television coverage, which they're not doing now. They can perform in front of the cameras and mikes. That's the only real objection I have to the present briefing system, other than that I'd prefer the two-a-day system. (There's

---

[50]Telephone interview with Pierpoint, August 6, 1979.

[51]Telephone interview with Ms. Compton, November 16, 1979.

[52]Correspondence with Ms. Woodruff, May 23, 1980.

now one daily session on weekdays; that was changed in the Nixon Era.)"[53]

Ms. Compton: "There was a time when the briefings were abused by some correspondents representing rather extreme views. I think it's most effective today when Jody is available at a certain time of day. (Rex Granum, his deputy, has never been given real authority.) I think the briefing plus access to Jody in his office is the best combination."[54]

Brokaw: "As for the briefing format, with the exception of the cameras not being present, I have very little trouble with it."[55]

Ms. Woodruff: "I think briefings are fine the way they are. . . . there are times, when I would like to have television coverage of all White House briefings but I suppose that would make Powell even more circumspect in his answers than he already is. What we need is more candor, not less!

"I understand the occasional need for deep background briefings, but I prefer them as seldom as possible."[56]

Each correspondent was asked how he or she had seen the White House Press Office change during his or her time in Washington and why.

Pierpoint: "It's changed relatively little in size, but the big change has not been in the Press Office but in the press corps, which has tripled in

---

[53]Telephone interview with Pierpoint, August 6, 1979.

[54]Telephone interview with Ms. Compton, November 16, 1979.

[55]Telephone interviews with Brokaw, December 10, 1979, and February 13, 1980.

[56]Correspondence with Ms. Woodruff, May 23, 1980.

size. Television has of course become the dominant medium and the Press Office has shifted its operations to meet that. I would say the press secretary's operation has probably changed less than that of most other institutions."[57]

Ms. Compton: "It has changed very little. The system is still the same. The people I dealt with when Ford came in were basically the same ones who were there when Nixon was there."[58]

Ms. Woodruff: "Powell has grown increasingly skillful at learning how to use the press . . . and how to play reporters off against one another . . . for his own purposes. I don't believe he is as skillful as he might be, however, because I think much of what he tries to achieve, is made public, and appears to be clumsy. But there is no doubt, that there is great use of the 'leak'. . . . and that occasionally it serves a purpose, for the White House's benefit."[59]

Another question dealt with the proper role of television in contributing to citizen knowledge and public information.

Pierpoint: "That's a pretty philosophical question. I think it should reflect the concerns of the public and pass them on to the White House and the President. Television should also try to pass on to the public along with the news as much background as possible to put the news in context."[60]

---

[57] Telephone interview with Pierpoint, August 6, 1979. This opinion represents an interesting parallel with that of George Christian who spoke of a "rut since Hagerty's time."

[58] Telephone interview with Ms. Compton, November 16, 1979.

[59] Woodruff correspondence, May 23, 1980.

[60] Telephone interview with Pierpoint, August 6, 1979.

Ms. Compton: "Television's big role is to let the American people get to know the President by seeing him close up with wrinkles under his eyes, etc. The public through television can see him at those big rallies and small meeting. This is the single most important role of television at the White House, or in relation to the President."[61]

Ms. Woodruff: "Television must serve a broad crosss-section of citizens. . . . the mass of the public . . . with varying amounts of education and intelligence, and therefore should not attempt, to talk over people's heads, with sophisticated subject matter that many people won't be able to understand. The smartest, best educated people, will turn to other sources for their news, as well, anyway. Having said that, I think the networks have in the past been guilty of underestimating the minds of the viewers . . . and that news coverage should be at as high a level as possible and still be understandable. We have a responsibility to inform people about news that affects their lives . . . news that is important to them . . . whether they realize it or not. We should no fall prey to just giving people what we think they 'want' to hear. It is important to remember, that television is the 'first line' of information . . . that it can be little more than the first, the top layer, of information . . . and that for in-depth understanding of issues, developments, trends, etc. . . . the public must turn to other sources . . . newspapers, magazines, books. Television is a rich source but it is not the only source. . . and it should whet viewers' appetites to turn elsewhere for more."[62]

Correspondents were asked whether a co-ordinated approach to information policy by federal agencies would be helpful to them, or whether this mattered at the White House level:

---

[61]Compton interview, November 16, 1979.

[62]Woodruff correspondence, May 23, 1980.

Pierpoint: "I don't know that I'd like to see better co-ordination in government, from our point of view. I consider heavy co-ordination a kind of Nixonian concept. It might not help the public's to know. I think the public gets more information the way things are now."[63]

Ms. Compton: "It would help more on Capitol Hill. At the White House you get everything through the White House Press Office. (For example, the Department of Transportation press office puts out material about a new mass transit plan in great detail. But the highlights are available through the White House Press Office. For our purposes, that's usually enough."[64]

Ms. Woodruff: "It would make the job easier, but it doesn't hurt to have to fish around among various agencies for information . . . it gives one a feel for how different agencies view and deal with issues and policy."[65]

Correspondents were asked to describe their participation in overseas coverage of the President. Some observations:

Pierpoint: "It's not that much different. You're still covering the President but your job is basically the same. The focus is on foreign affairs, it's true, but we're generalists anyway. Sometimes problems exist. It may be more difficult to have access to information and to get information out to the public. There are some differences. Because of time-zone differences, you may work an 18-hour day overseas. In other ways, it's not much different than traveling domestically. The White House still charters a plane and the network pays. It takes more

---

[63] Pierpoint interview, August 6, 1979.

[64] Compton interview, November 16, 1979.

[65] Woodruff correspondence, May 23, 1980.

212

manpower."[66]

Ms. Compton: "We are somewhat captives of Jody's
even more than in Washington. At the economic summit
in Bonn, we were half a city away from the sessions.
You have very limited access, for example, to (Zbig-
niew) Brzezinski and you have to rely more on Jody
and the White House Press Office."[67]

Ms. Woodruff: "I have covered every presidential trip overseas, except for his first . . . a trip
to London, for an economic summit, in early 1977.
All the others, I've been deeply involved in!"[68]

Finally, each correspondent was asked whether
traveling to cover the President or Vice President
overseas is something he or she enjoys. These were
their comments:

Pierpoint: "I don't enjoy the travel that much
because of the tremendous workload and time that's
involved. We usually try to cover in infinite detail
when the President is traveling overseas, more so
than when he's at home. I tend to consider it a
chore, a burden. When I was a foreign correspondent,
I loved to travel. There are some exceptions to this,
of course. If you can go ahead of the President's
party, as I recently did in Tokyo, and have more time
to do the coverage, that's different. But you're
working long hours every day under normal circumstances."[69]

Ms. Compton: "They treat you awfully well.
The press plane is comfortable. Your baggage is
picked up and delivered to your hotel, right outside
your room. I've had dinner in the basement of the
Palace at Versailles; I've seen castles in Spain,

---

[66]Pierpoint interview, August 6, 1979.

[67]Compton interview, November 16, 1979.

[68]Woodruff correspondence, May 23, 1980.

[69]Pierpoint interview, August 6, 1979.

and walked the Great Wall of China. What more can one want?"[70]

Ms. Woodruff: "I enjoy the companionship of my colleagues . . . I enjoy getting to see places I would never otherwise get to see . . . and I enjoy being able to witness, first hand, the reaction of other people . . . ordinary citizens, and other officials . . . U. S. and foreign . . . to the President. I also enjoy observing a part of history . . . and covering a trip gives reporters more access to the President, than when he stays in the White House.

"I don't enjoy being a slave to the White House. agenda. . . having to travel in 'packs' . . . and not being able to move among the crowds . . . or get physically to other locations, where I may talk personally with other key governmental or political figures."[71]

By chance, a Philadelphia reporter-documentary producer with the Public Broadcasting Service expressed a willingness to co-operate in my research, and his views give an interesting counterpoint to the views of White House "regulars". Don Fouser of WHYY, Philadelphia, had the following comments:

"I feel that such intimacy with the White House daily, indeed weekly and yearly, means a submersion of self into the office-personality of another. I would consider it demeaning to simply cover the White House. Yet it is a 'trip' for press who are there. It means thay get on air (TV) every night. A Dan Rather becomes a national name and 'hero'. . . . The same gold leaf rubs off on anyone associated with the White House as I have found out in my perambulations. Ask any presidential assistant of the past and he will readily admit that it was a heady experience to be in the big white house. George Reedy writes about it "Twilight". Though his ex-

---

[70]Compton interview, November 16, 1979.

[71]Woodruff correspondence, May 23, 1980.

perience was distorted (his only experience being with LBJ and that is <u>unique</u>), it reflects honestly about what happens to those who are in and about the White House--and this includes journalists. So I think we get a distorted view of the Presidency and what it means to the world and indeed to the U. S. public. I am more affected by the selectmen and school committee members in my daily life than by most Presidents."[72]

"My limited contact with (the White House) indicates: (1) that I can never get Jody Powell to answer a call; (2) that the only way to get response from the White House is to be in the '<u>star</u>' category. White House access is dismal at best for most press.

"(Television) is still headline. And time given to presidential activities is all out of proportion to its importance in our system. The reason is that it is easier--takes fewer man hours--to cover presidential activity. Congress takes a big commitment from any news gathering organization.

"Three-on-one is again artificial. It suits the three 'commercial' networks and no one else. And yet the President is trapped by seemingly having to be fair to each of them. This is baloney. You know it; I know it. The public knows it. But it has become a convention. The public suffers from such network pressures.

"I have no complaints about how Powell does his job.

"I produce all sorts of programs: variety, drama, documentary, etc. My knowledge of and experience with covering the Presidency or the White House is limited.

---

[72]Correspondence with author, November 16, 1979. Mr. Fouser was affiliated with production of a PBS documentary series, "Every Four Years", with Howard K. Smith.

"A White House correspondent should cover the hard breaking news originating from the office of the President, not concern himself with trivia, and interpret what he/she has learned. But the job is myopic and to a correspondent on this beat the Presidency seems the center of the universe, which it is not.

(Regarding new technology in communications) "There are two questions here. One answer is that changes in TV technology will change access to the public and for producers of softwear. Coverage of the Presidency will not change until attitudes of reporters change.

"I prefer informal background press 'conferences' without cameras, without still photographs and without any hoopla. Then I respect the journalists reporting about such a 'conference'. The rest is hooey, non productive except for a President who wants air time and networks who wish to fill air time.

(One institutionalization of the Press Office) "Since FDR it has become institutionalized. I am not sure that such daily access to Presidents is essential or desirable.

"Television so far covers events and does it superbly. For information one needs to read. There is no substitute. TV is least efficient in transmitting information and cannot (should not) be relied on."

Mr. Fouser found it made no difference whether federal agency information policies were co-ordinated. He also commented about traveling with Presidents for news coverage: "I don't and I wouldn't."[73]

---

[73]Questionaire comments from Don Fouser, WHYY, December 1979.

Thus newspaper and broadcast correspondents' views of White House coverage can be compared. In the final chapter I will draw conclusions about various aspects of White House news coverage.

CHAPTER FIFTEEN

CONCLUSIONS ABOUT WHITE HOUSE PRESS OFFICE

AND PRESS SECRETARIES

Evolution and _Development_ of the _Office_--The office of White House Press Secretary can be said to have gone through three major periods in its evolution and development. These are: (1) the period of dominance by newspapers and magazines; (2) the period of the heyday of radio coverage; (3) the modern period of dominance by television coverage. Later I will discuss the impact of television on image-building, and insert some reservations about opinion leaders' exposure to the print media which serves to qualify the temptation toward sweeping generalities about television.

The first reference to a Press Secretary serving in the position somewhat as it is now conceived of, was made by the late President Herbert Hoover, who referred in his _Memoirs_ to George Akerson as one of several special secretaries, who attended to the press.[1]

An earlier White House secretary, part of whose duties included dealings with the press, was Joseph P. Tumulty, a secretary to President Wilson, who sometimes was obliged to smooth things over

---

[1]The _Memoirs_ of Herbert Hoover: The _Cabinet_ and the _Presidency_: 1920-1933 (New York: Macmillan, 1952), pp. 218-219.

with the press for the President.[2] Preceding
Wilson, Presidents had not yet developed the
institution of the press conference, although
Theodore Roosevelt met informally with reporters
and correspondents and was considered unusually
accessible by previous standards.

Presidents who usually dealt with the press
through a spokesman who also had other duties
included William Howard Taft, Warren G. Harding
and Calvin Coolidge. Persons such as Everett
Sanders and Bascom Slemp served Coolidge as
secretaries, but his press relations never moved
beyond the rather formal use of a spokesman. The
usual practice during this time (including the
Hoover era) was to require that questions be
presented in writing.

While Coolidge and Harding, and to some extent
Hoover made perfunctory use of radio to communicate
with the public in addresses, the dominant media
of this era were clearly the print media--newspaper
editorial endorsements carried great weight, and
the institution of the syndicated column had not
yet grown to have the tremendous effect which it
did in the 1930's and 1940's.

The New York _Times_ and newspapers of that
character were read avidly in Washington, and staff
aides of Presidents were interested in securing
the best coverage possible in the newspapers, as
well as of course securing editorial endorsements
at campaign time.

It was said of Theodore Roosevelt in the era
when newspaper coverage really counted, that he

---

[2]For a more detailed discussion of Tumulty's
dealings with the press, see John Morton Blum, _Joe
Tumulty and the Wilson Era_ (Boston: Houghton
Mifflin Co., 1951), pp. 61-65. Tumulty is described
by Blum as "the first Secretary to have a flair for
public relations" (p. 61).

devised the approach of releasing much of his news over the weekend when it had the least competition for attention. This supposedly accounted for a greater focus on White House actions in the Sunday and especially Monday morning newspapers.

This was an era when Extras were published, when newspaper correspondents received great acclaim. Even the advent of commercial radio in the 1920's did not bring this epoch to an immediate end.

Instead the great forward strides of radio came in the 1930's when Franklin D. Roosevelt, a President who recognized its potential, made use of it in the "fireside chat" which he delivered at infrequent intervals. He combined this with the informal press conference held as often as twice weekly and so designed that on some occasions morning papers would receive the news first and on other occasions evening papers would do so.[3]

Roosevelt was served by Marvin McIntyre as appointments secretary and by Stephen Early as press secretary. Early and the President often had an informal briefing session prior to the 10:30 a.m. presidential press conferences.

An early meeting of FDR with four correspondents and Stephen Early in 1933 is recounted by Frank Freidel. The Press Secretary met the reporters in the Red Room and took them upstairs to the new

---

[3]For a more detailed discussion of Roosevelt's use of the press conference and fireside chats, see Elmer E. Cornwell Jr., Presidential Leadership of Public Opinion (Bloomington, IN: Indiana University Press, 1965).

President's study where FDR read them his proclamation of a banking holiday.[4]

On Wednesday, March 8, 1933, at 10:10 a.m.
FDR met with 125 newspapermen in the Oval Office.
Direct quotations were not permitted unless Early
provided correspondents with statements in writing.
But there was much use of "background information".[5]

FDR in his reading usually examined the New
York _Times_ and _Herald_ _Tribune_, the Washington _Post_
and _Herald_, and the Baltimore _Sun_. He was particularly attentive to columns by Frank Kent and
Walter Lippmann in this period.[6] He held press
conferences of 15 to 30 minutes duration, and the
atmosphere has been described as relaxed. Friedel
comments: "Roosevelt treated the newspapermen as
though they were all junior members of an exclusive
club, something like the Fly Club had been at
Harvard--but with him presiding as the benign
senior, ready to join in the fun, but just a trifle
aloof."[7]

Early's background was that of a Virginian with
long experience with the Associated Press. Along
with McIntyre he had worked for FDR in the 1920
campaign.[8]

Toward the end of Roosevelt's tenure and the
beginning of the Truman era, radio had come into
its own. It perhaps came of age with the crises

---

[4]Frank Freidel, _FDR: Launching the New Deal_
(Boston: Little, Brown, 1973), p. 216.

[5]Freidel, _op. cit._, p. 224.

[6]Freidel, _op. cit._, pp. 274-275.

[7]Freidel, _op. cit._, p. 279.

[8]Arthur Schlesinger Jr., _The Coming of the New_
Deal (Boston: Houghton, Mifflin, 1939), p. 516.

prior to World War II and World War II itself, which focused attention on instantaneous reports from such newsmen and analysts as Edward R. Murrow, H. V. Kaltenborn and William L. Shirer.

It now became possible for brief excerpts from President's comments, when authorized, to be played in recorded form for the radio networks' news programs.

The first Press Secretary to serve Harry Truman was Charles Ross, known to most newsmen as Charley, and he had a long and distinguished journalistic background. He became Washington bureau chief for the St. Louis Post-Dispatch in 1918, and had worked in the field of education prior to that. He was a classmate of Harry Truman at Independence High School, where he was valedictorian. A 1905 graduate of the University of Missouri School of Journalism, Ross worked on Colorado and Missouri newspapers before teaching for 10 years at Missouri. One year he was in Melbourne, Australia, as visiting editor of the Melbourne Herald. Ross won a Pulitzer Prize during the first of two periods in the Washington bureau, and he returned to the capital after working for a time on the Post-Dispatch editorial page staff. Robert S. Allen and William V. Shannon felt Ross was more outstanding as a correspondent than as Press Secretary.[9]

Joseph Short succeeded Ross as Truman's Press Secretary. He had not been in the post long when he was obliged to announce the momentous news that the President had fired General Douglas MacArthur from his command in the Far East in April 1951.

Truman's final Press Secretary was Roger Tubby, who was referred to earlier when mention was made

---

[9]Allen and Shannon, The Truman Merry-Go-Round (New York: Vanguard Press, 1950), pp. 54-55.

of him in quoting from an interview with Pierre Salinger.

The Truman era saw the public turn increasingly to radio for information about the President, but most felt that President Truman used radio less effectively than Roosevelt. But the news conference format was quite similar to that under Roosevelt, with Truman holding conferences at first in the Oval Office and later in the Indian Treaty Room of the Executive Office Building.

This period also saw the beginning of the growth of television; mostly an East Coast phenomenon in 1948 when Truman ran for election in his own right, television had become linked in coast-to-coast fashion with coaxial cables by 1951 when the signing of the Japanese peace treaty in San Francisco was the first major news event covered by nationwide TV. Even though President Truman used this medium for addresses and even though TV correspondents were accredited by 1953, at the end of the Truman period, it had not yet come fully into its own and would not really do so until midway of the Johnson era.

Eisenhower's Press Secretary, James C. Hagerty, was the first to permit filming of news conferences and the broadcasting of portions of these conferences on television. By the end of his Administration in 1961, Eisenhower had moved close to live television coverage, but the final transition had not yet been made. Hagerty incidentally as noted in an earlier chapter came to the White House from a newspaper background and service with Governor Dewey.

During Eisenhower's time some experimentation was done with television, such as a staged Cabinet meeting for the small screen, and some use of live television was made outside the news conference format. Radio and the print media still remained important during this era.

With John F. Kennedy, the full-dress, live televised news conference came into its own. And television was approaching the time when it drew a larger audience for political news than any other medium.

Pierre Salinger served effectively as Kennedy's press secretary. He had known the President prior to his campaign, as did most of the Kennedy staff. Salinger's experience prior to the White House had been with the San Francisco Chronicle, Collier's, the two Adlai Stevenson presidential campaigns (as a press aide), and the Senate Labor Rackets Committee. Robert Kennedy was counsel for the committee and Senator John F. Kennedy was a member. Salinger, like Hagerty in 1952, had worked in the 1960 Kennedy presidential campaign.

Lyndon Johnson's White House period was marked by three new Press Secretaries, much controversy over Vietnam, and a never-ending search for an appropriate format for news conferences. Correspondence examined in the Johnson Library indicates that he finally found this in November 1967 during an indoor news conference when for the first time he used a "lavalier" microphone which made it possible for him to avoid being anchored to a podium. Most observers felt he was quite effective in this sense, but within a few months he had made his announcement that he would not be a candidate in 1968.

By this time television had clearly become the dominant medium. This was already beginning to happen when as David Halberstam reports President Kennedy began seeing less of such magazine correspondents as Hugh Sidey of Time and began seeing more of such network correspondents as Sander Vanocur of NBC.

Johnson's preoccupation with news coverage is also noteworthy. Johnson kept three monitors in the oval office, so that he could follow network

newscasts at will if he so desired. Lest this be
thought a strange whim, it ought to be pointed out
that the Johnson family had once held the controlling
interest in the Austin television station and had
long been interested in the broadcasting industry.
While President Kennedy, whose media relations
were basically good, occasionally did such things
as ostracizing Ben Bradlee of Newsweek for several
weeks, canceling his subscription to the New York
Herald Tribune and requesting the New York Times
to reassign Halberstam somewhere other than South
Vietnam, his preoccupation with the media was
considerably less than that of President Johnson. [10]

The Johnson Press Secretaries were George
Reedy, Bill Moyers, and George Christian. Christian
is currently in public relations in Texas, Moyers
is now with the Public Broadcasting Service in
New York, and Reedy is Nieman Professor of
Journalism at Marquette University. Reedy and
Christian had previous journalistic experience.

Richard Nixon employed Ronald Ziegler as his
Press Secretary and Herbert Klein as his Communications Director during most of his five-year
tenure. Nixon was known for an antagonistic
attitude toward the news media, and he held news
conferences quite infrequently. Some of the
efforts made by the Nixon Administration against
the media have been documented. [11]

------

[10] In my The Presidency and the Mass Media in
the Age of Television (Washington: University Press
of America, 1978), I quoted from memos prepared by
Johnson aides who sent them to the President
through the Press Secretary. All dealt with contacts with media persons.

[11] See William E. Porter, Assault on the Media:
The Nixon Years (Ann Arbor, Michigan: University
of Michigan Press, 1977).

Besides the President, those who castigated the media included Vice President Spiro T. Agnew, Chief of Staff H. R. Haldeman, and Clay T. Whitehead, who was director of the Office of Telecommunications Policy. The President also had a Houston confrontation with Dan Rather of CBS which made the public react considerably in 1973.

When Ziegler had to describe some previous statements as "inoperative" during the Watergate period, Nixon finally placed him in Klein's old job and Gerald Warren served as acting Press Secretary. Ziegler also went to San Clemente with Nixon at the beginning of his retirement. Ziegler, like Haldeman and others in the Nixon Administration, had basically an advertising agency background. Klein however had been a member of the working press.

Gerald Ford struck controversy when his first Press Secretary, Jerald R. terHorst, had been with him less than a month. TerHorst resigned because of the pardon of former President Nixon. His background had been that of a Washington correspondent for the Detroit News and he returned to that position after resigning. Ford's second and last Press Secretary, Ronald Nessen, had been an NBC correspondent and prior to that was a wire reporter. He is now a free lancer.

During the Nixon and Ford periods, new formats were developed for presidential news conferences outside Washington. Ford had better relations with the media than Nixon, but as is true with most presidents, he had his bad moments as well.

Jimmy Carter's "born again" Baptist background intrigued the media during the 1976 campaign much as John Kennedy's Catholicism had attracted its attention during the 1960 campaign. Carter also quickly developed an "anti-Washington" or "outsider" image during the campaign which caused him some difficulties later.

227

Carter was well served however by having a Press Secretary in Jody Powell who had been with him for many years and was able to convey the President's authentic views. Various other responsibilities in this area have been handled for Carter by the television adviser, Barry Jagoda, for two years, and later by an assistant for communications, Gerald Rafshoon, who handled the Carter media campaign in 1976 and was developing it for 1980 at this writing.

Carter was suffering from a poor press image during early 1978 and much of 1979, but the Camp David Summit and the Iranian crisis interrupted periods of low standing in the polls.

Perhaps the most noteworthy thing about the Carter press operation is that it has been of necessity larger than those of earlier Presidents, partly because of the mushrooming growth of the Washington correspondent corps.

A final word needs to be said here about the impact of television on image-building. "Jimmy Who" might never have received the nomination nor won the election without it; Senator Kennedy, his chief 1980 challenger, might have made a better start except for a weak television interview with Roger Mudd on Chappaquiddick. The outcome in 1980 was clouded as of this writing.

Rating the Effectiveness of Press Secretaries--It is possible to develop an ideal type for two kinds of Press Secretaries. These would be the Technicians and the Policy Advisers.

Technicians see their job as conveying the news to the public and they either choose not to go beyond that, or their Presidents seem to prefer for them not to do so.

Policy Advisers are those who are so essential to the smooth working of their Presidents' White House management task that they serve in a kind of dual role--both Press Secretary and intimate adviser.

228

This is all by way of prefacing some observations on the effectiveness of Press Secretaries.

Journalists seemed almost unanimous in the belief that the effectiveness of a Press Secretary is almost in direct relationship to the degree to which the President feels it possible to confide in him sufficiently to allow the Press Secretary to accurately reflect the President's views.

Judged by this standard the most effective Press Secretaries since Roosevelt's time probably have been Stephen Early, James C. Hagerty, George Christian, and Jody Powell. There is considerable testimony that each of these men has been able to reflect their President's views accurately, or to put it as Marquis Childs did, "their principal's views".

This generalization should be illustrated by two examples, those of Hagerty and Powell. Evidence indicates that in Hagerty's case, he was relied on by the President for advice even though he has suggested that this could be overstated. He clearly had a most important role at the time that President Eisenhower suffered a heart attack in 1955.

In the case of Jody Powell, from the beginnings of the Carter Administration up to the Iranian crisis, it has been felt that the two staff members closest to the President have been Chief of Staff Hamilton Jordan and Powell. This has been reflected in the way in which Powell's statements are conveyed in the media. As the ABC correspondent Ann Compton so well stated it, the fact that Powell has been with President Carter since 1966 and knows his thinking so well is bound to carry credence with the news media.

Why have some capable men rated less well with the media? George Reedy and Ron Ziegler are both examples, although the media obviously had greater respect for the former. For whatever reason,

President Johnson did not feel able to confide in Reedy as Press Secretary to the same extent he did when Reedy was a member of the LBJ staff on Capitol Hill. This was not Reedy's doing but it caused difficulties for him with the media. In Ziegler's case, it was felt that his job was downgraded by the Nixon Administration and his low standing with the media was partly a reflection of the President's attitude. But it was felt that unlike Reedy's case, the background of Ziegler did not adequately prepare him for the job.

With these examples in mind, it is possible to state as almost an ironclad rule of White House media relations:

The effectiveness of any Press Secretary lies in his ability to speak accurately for his President. It does not seem to be necessary to elaborate further on this, in view of the previous discussion.

Despite the factor of easy access by Press Secretaries to important and solid information, there are some difficulties which arise when a Press Secretary is part of the White House "inner circle".

The principal difficulty seems to be that when the Press Secretary is in frequent consultation with the President or other key aides, a problem of access arises for White House correspondents. There seems to be little that can be done about this problem. It almost can be said that this is the price correspondents pay for knowing they are getting authentic information.

Correspondents at the White House also note that the flood of presidential activities made it difficult sometimes to sort out the wheat from the chaff in news coverage. This was mentioned by both Cormier and Ms. Compton in their interviews. Perhaps greater resources and the use of additional correspondents to get supple-

mentary information from outside the White House
may be a better approach to this problem from the
journalists' point of view.

From the viewpoint of Press Secretaries and
the White House, the first object of the whole
media operation is to get the President's views
effectively before the public. In the Iranian
crisis this has occurred, although State Department
officials like Hodding Carter III and Tom Reston
have shared the limelight with Powell during this
situation. Some felt that the Carter Administration's greatest difficulty in getting the
President's views across came with the Lance case
and the "domestic summit" at Camp David. Critics
said this might have been avoided by better
preparing the public, but it should always be
remembered that information later becomes
available that sometimes explains seeming
discrepancies such as these.

Future Prospects for Office of Press Secre-
tary--While at least one Washington correspondent
described the job as an almost impossible one,
it seems likely that the position of the Press
Secretary is likely to remain a crucial one for
some time to come.

The explanation for this is partly because
of the changing relationship between institutions
of a political character. In today's television
age, with satellite communication bringing
instant news of events around the globe, the
media play a significant part in shaping the
public's views of leaders and events. This
makes the necessity for an effective Press
Secretary even more crucial for any President.

Certain landmarks in Press Secretaries'
practices have been evident and have left a
legacy to be handed down to the future Press
Secretaries. One of these was the comprehensive
briefing approach to the job taken by James C.

231

Hagerty. Another was the introduction of live television by Pierre Salinger. Still others have occurred with Ziegler, Nessen and Powell in wider use of a nation-wide approach to reaching the people at the grass roots rather than relying on traditional Washington news reportage.

The Washington correspondent corps will always be crucial, but there seems to be a lag in Press Office services to support the kind of extensive grass-roots contacts that modern Presidents seem to be moving toward. This was pointed out by Frank Cormier, who has a base of nearly two decades of White House reporting to use as a basis of comparison.

What are future Press Secretaries likely to do with prospective technology? This may depend more on the media themselves than on Press Secretaries. Already satellites, use of terminals and other innovations have been accepted as commonplace. It is difficult to project very far ahead in considering this question. But it is reasonable to say that Press Secretaries will use whatever technology they believe will get the President's views out to the public better than in the past.

Significance of the Office to Modern Presidents--When it is pointed out that Presidents did not even have staff assistance until 1857, that they labored long with merely a private secretary, and that the first man to hold the title of Press Secretary in even an ad hoc fashion was appointed in 1929, a clearer idea of the evolution of the office of Press Secretary is possible.

However, in recent administrations the need for the President to delegate this portion of his responsibilities to a Press Secretary has increased rather than diminished. As Pierre Salinger noted, "President Kennedy could have been his own Press Secretary if he had had the time".

But alas Presidents run up against a finite limit to their time; even Press Secretaries do so.

The relationship of media imagery (in which the Press Secretary by the nature of things is inevitably bound up) with perishable ratings in public opinion polls is a puzzle faced by modern Presidents. They must use the image-making machinery; conversely they deal with a public that seems increasingly cynical about it. Poll ratings may not be affected by instant imagery, but past image-making efforts may leave a residue that affects them. Certainly they have an impact on the public's expectations of what any President will achieve in office.

The question may also be asked: Do the media themselves promote public doubts and cynicism about Presidents? The answer may be a qualified yes, but it has to be considered in the context of the fact that the media view themselves as performing a necessary watchdog role for public officials.

Is this a healthy or an unhealthy development for the public's relationship with its Presidents? It could be a healthy development if cynicism is not carried too far, if the public begins to develop realistic expectations about what Presidents and their staffs can achieve or not achieve.

Summary Comments--It has been demonstrated that the evolution of the office of Press Secretary, while gradual, has been a vital aspect in the modern Presidency. It has also been suggested that a typology of Press Secretaries can be developed, with the two principal categories those of Technicians and Policy Advisers. It has also been suggested that present institutional developments will make the Press Secretary more, rather than less, important to future Presidents.

The outlook is that Presidents will choose their Press Secretaries from now on with great care.

And well they might, because the Press Secretary stands at that crucial point of initial contact between the President and the public in many instances. Even when the President speaks to the public without a mediating figure like the Press Secretary, he has doubtless sought his advice.

Thus this appointive office has grown increasingly in importance and stature. It is likely to continue to do so.

241

ABOUT THE AUTHOR

WILLIAM C. SPRAGENS, Visiting Professor at the American University, on leave as Associate Professor at Bowling Green State University, Bowling Green, Ohio, is the co-author of Conflict and Crisis in American Politics (with Robert W. Russell, now of the U. S. Senate staff) and author of The Presidency and the Mass Media in the Age of Television. He has contributed chapters to Joseph S. Roucek, ed., Contemporary Aspects of Geopolitics; William C. Adams, ed., Television News and the Middle East; Bradley D. Nash, ed., Organizing and Staffing the White House, all forthcoming, and two earlier volumes. A recipient of a Moody Grant from the Lyndon Baines Johnson Foundation in 1978 and 1979, a National Endowment for the Humanities Summer Fellowship in 1978, and grants from the National Science Foundation and the Law Enforcement Assistance Agency as well as other grants, he has been an active researcher since earning the Ph. D. in political science at Michigan State University. Earlier academic appointments were at the University of Tennessee, Millikin University and Wisconsin State University. A career as journalist preceding his academic career included positions with the Dayton Journal Herald, Fort Wayne Journal-Gazette and Lexington Herald. He served on the staff at the 1978 Democratic Mid-Term Conference in Memphis, has attended five national nominating conventions with field work projects, and is currently working on a volume on imagery and the Presidency and a basic textbook on the American Presidency.

243